HOW TO
Draw Cars
LIKE A PRO

Thom Taylor with Lisa Hallett

MBI Publishing Company

First published in 1996 by MBI Publishing Company, PO Box 1, 729 Prospect Avenue, Osceola, WI 54020-0001 USA

MBI Publishing Company books are also available at discounts in bulk quantity for industrial or sales-promotional use. For details write to Special Sales Manager at Motorbooks International Wholesalers & Distributors, 729 Prospect Avenue, PO Box 1, Osceola, WI 54020-0001 USA.

Library of Congress Cataloging-in-Publication Data

Taylor, Thom.
    How to draw cars like a pro / Thom Taylor.
      p. cm.
    Includes index.
    ISBN 0-7603-0010-0   (pbk. : alk. paper)
      1. Automobiles in art.   2. Drawing—Technique.   I. Title.
    NC825.A8T39   1996
    743. '89629222—dc21   96-51114

On the front cover: Thom Taylor's sketch of the Pete Chapouris Group/ *Street Rodder* magazine Hot 1940 Ford Coupe.

On the frontispiece: Steve Stanford drew this radical Bug for *Hot VWs* magazine.

On the title page: This stretched and chopped coupe is another Thom Taylor original.

On the back cover: Top: Steve Stanford created this low, low cruiser. Bottom: A radical drop top is used to demonstrate different drawing techniques.

Printed in China

Contents

Acknowledgments

I blame this whole thing on author and friend Tony Thacker who, upon feeling there was a need, and having sold Motorbooks on the idea, encouraged me to do a book concentrating on the basics of drawing cars. He told me he'd write it if I would lend technical information, do the diagrams, and provide the art. Well, one thing led to another and before long we were two years down the road, and Tony was on to other interesting projects and pursuits. Motorbooks still wanted the book. So, with the skillful hands and know-how of my lovely wife, Lisa, who has a B.A. in art and is a professional writer and editor, we pressed on.

All along, I wanted to pass on the fantastic automotive art of my colleagues and, in most cases, friends, to the reader. I'm proud to be presenting 14 artists or designers other than myself. All were very giving of their time and art, and I don't feel this book would be the best it could be without their inclusion. I admire their work a great deal and have probably "borrowed" a thing or two from each of these guys at one time or another. Maybe you will, too. Thanks, guys!

Three artists from this group I would like to thank in particular are Tom West, Ed Golden, and Jim Bruni. All three went through a great amount of time to explain their respective techniques, and I really appreciate their efforts and encouragement.

Art Center College of Design really forced my ability to draw and design cars, but it was the enthusiast magazines of my youth and the artists featured in them that really sparked my desire to learn to draw cars. That is one of the underlying reasons I do so much magazine work today. Those featured creative individuals include Tom Medley, Joe Henning, Harry Bradley, Tom Daniel, Larry Wood, and Kenny Youngblood. They're all still around, still creating, and still influencing me. They probably have had a great influence on many people. I'm fortunate to be allowed this space to thank them.

Those dog-eared old car magazines also exposed me to some really fabulous car artists I want to mention. Painters and pinstripers all, they include Larry Watson, Dean Jeffries, Ed "Big Daddy" Roth, and Von Dutch. The significance of their contributions to automobile culture is only now becoming apparent, though I believe they have always been appreciated.

Before we get off the magazine subject, I would like to thank all the editors, art directors, and publishers who have given me both encouragement and, more importantly, money. Although I get involved with numerous design and graphics projects, this has been my bread and butter for many years. A special thanks to John Dianna of Petersen Publishing, who has been a faithful friend and source of projects over the last 10 or so years, and who allowed me to pull from their files for a few examples of my illustrations.

For the parents of a budding car artist, you must know all your support and encouragement are needed for a child with such a "different" interest as this. To that end, I especially thank my parents, Charles and Ann Taylor, who early on and to this day offer much encouragement and enthusiasm for their son's quirky profession.

Though I mentioned my wife early on for her help with this book, I would like to thank her and son Jamie for enduring my strong focus on this book in the final weeks of its gestation. I love you both.

Now, let's draw some cars.

Introduction

A prominent Los Angeles surgeon I know once told me the less the medical profession knows about something, the more they write about it. That is why they could have filled a large room with books on polio before Jonas Salk discovered a cure. Now, polio only rates a paragraph in medical textbooks. I wondered if the opposite applies to drawing cars? I see poorly drawn cars in magazines, books, and advertising all the time. Maybe I notice it more because I'm such a car nut and it's what I do for a living.

Looking through the art libraries and book stores periodically, I see lots of information on architectural design and rendering, graphics, even fashion and computer illustration. Drawing cars is a little bit of all of these and more, but nothing exists to expose this fun and exciting activity. Maybe the reason there is so little about how to illustrate cars has something to do with their being so dynamic. Just the plethora of car styles, and the shapes and sculpturing within those styles, can be intimidating. Add to this color, environment, time of day, direction of the light, and finishes on the surface of a car's body, and illustrating an automobile becomes complex.

Back when I was taking art classes in high school and college—before starting Art Center—obtaining information on drawing cars was like sex: highly desired but impossible to get. I think art teachers looked upon it as a skill much like refinishing furniture or laying bricks, as opposed to an artistic endeavor. But to be honest, I think at least part of this was due to their inability to do it themselves. There is nothing wrong with that, but as a result, my learning the intricacies of car illustration was left up to my own observations, devices, and, ultimately, my own frustrations.

So, before you is my earnest attempt to make this dirty little secret more attainable. A lot of information gets covered in just over 100 pages, so I chose to leave a few things out. I don't get into painting or airbrush illustration. I felt the focus should be on drawing itself and the simpler techniques of rendering before tackling these more rigorous methods. And besides, there are numerous books and magazines covering airbrush art and the process of painting that can be applied to cars once you know the information provided here, so I make no apologies for omitting these specific techniques.

One other thing not covered in this book: Your mistakes become your successes, because you learn what not to do, which helps lead to the path of knowing how *to* do it. My father told me early on that the mark of a great artist was one who could make a mistake look like it was meant to be there. I don't know what an accountant was doing advising his son on art, but he was right. Even if you can't make good out of the bad line, mark, or sketch, you most likely won't make that mistake again.

Drawing cars should be fun, but as with anything rewarding, it takes dedication to become really proficient. What out there worth doing doesn't? With a few shortcuts provided here and the desire to do it, you can pick up the basics quickly. Hopefully, this will give you the impetus to continue on. Practice and observation are the keys.

For those who pick up the basics offered in this book, there is a chapter on professional schools and one on the burgeoning world of computer illustration and design. It is a frontier I'm just now entering, but one that I look forward to because of my solid drawing abilities. These are abilities I feel were more learned than endowed, which leads me to the conclusion that anyone can learn to draw as well as those featured in this book.

A Quick History in Automobile Design

Except for a few amateur inventors who may have fastened a crude steam engine to a couple of bicycles in attempts to come up with horseless contraptions, most people who design vehicles—whether for land, sea, or air—started with a pen to paper. It's a basic that's there from the get-go: An idea must be drawn to give engineers and designers, actually all of whom are involved in a vehicle's development, an opportunity to see what the ultimate product will look like. And the ability to draw a car is the first link in a long and circuitous chain.

Before you attack the drawing board with all those ultra-futuristic ideas you hope will wow them in Detroit in the 21st century, stop to consider how automobiles and you—if you want to get philosophical—got here. (Your dad probably went on a few dates with your mom before they got hitched, and he most likely needed a car to do so. Get it?) To understand why cars look the way they do, it is imperative that you know how the automobile evolved from its humble beginnings in the late 1800s to its high-tech forms of today.

In its infant stages, the automobile was just a motorized horse-drawn carriage sans the horse. These motorized buggies took on all of their forefathers' characteristics—from simple, open buggies to the more elaborate closed versions resembling horse-drawn coaches. They stuffed their motors or engines under the body close to the rear axle, thus becoming the drive-axle. Just after the turn of the century, builders started to position the engine up front ahead of a flat board to protect the passengers from the oil, smoke, and noise. Known as a firewall, this board became a perfect place to attach a windscreen, or windshield, and instruments with which to monitor the engine functions. This changed the horse-drawn-coach look that automobile makers had adopted, and ushered in the beginnings of what would become the more-recognized automobile layout of today, with a frame mounting an engine up front, followed by a firewall and body behind.

Americans liked the idea of getting around on their own. Automobile manufacturers quickly popped up across the country, particularly in the Midwest and Northeast. As demand increased for the convenient and versatile automobile, car

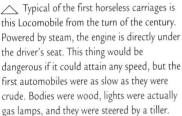 Typical of the first horseless carriages is this Locomobile from the turn of the century. Powered by steam, the engine is directly under the driver's seat. This thing would be dangerous if it could attain any speed, but the first automobiles were as slow as they were crude. Bodies were wood, lights were actually gas lamps, and they were steered by a tiller.

▽ This 1909 Overland touring was just a bigger, beefier version of the spindly Model T. The transition away from doorless bodies was fairly complete by 1912. Many companies, including Overland, were either absorbed by larger companies such as General Motors, or went out of business around the time of the Depression.

△ Model Ts like this 1910 roadster brought the automobile to the masses—they literally put America on the road. Compare this to the Locomobile to see how much cars changed in just a few years. Ford made running changes to this basic layout through the 1920s. Though very basic, this is essentially the layout for all cars right up to today.

builders concentrated on the manufacturing and development of mass-production techniques, as pioneered by industrialists such as Henry Ford and Ransom E. Olds. With this focus on the mechanical and manufacturing, the car's appearance often took a back seat. Yet, as business died out for the carriage trade, many of the remaining body suppliers shifted gears and started doing business with automobile manufacturers; some became automobile manufacturers themselves. Among the new selling points for both the body builders and, ultimately, the car manufacturers, were refinements for ease of manufacturing and passenger comfort, but also for the look or "flow" of the body

▷ By the 1920s, notice how smooth the bodies have gotten. Styling was starting to take a part in the marketing and perceived value of a car. The French-built Hispano-Suiza touring shown here is sporting a polished aluminum hood, dual side-mounted tires, and a 37.2-horsepower 6-cylinder engine.

▽ One of the truly classic makes was Duesenberg, represented here by this early 1930s phaeton. Notice the refinement of the body and how the fenders are starting to become longer and more flowing in an attempt to visually lengthen and lower the form.

surfaces and body joints. Even companies such as Ford, with its culture-changing Model T, were making running improvements to the appearances of its products.

By the mid-1920s, appearance or style became as much a customer preference as speed, comfort, versatility, and overall size. Styling sold cars. As welding and sheet-metal-forming processes developed, builders could do more with the body of a car. Nowhere was this more important than at General Motors, where in 1927 the company started its Art and Color section under the guidance of Harley Earl. With this step, GM had placed automobile styling as an equal to engineering and manufacturing in the development of an automobile. Styling soon would be a dominant factor in that process. This, combined with the "streamlined" revolution of the 1930s, led to the first golden age of automobile design.

Proportion, grace, and the sense of speed (or moving-while-standing-still) prompted lower bodies and tops, pontoon fenders more integrated to the body, and wind-swept windshields and radiators. Long hoods, combined with fastback rooflines, brought about a racy or fast look to automobiles including Duesenbergs, Pierce-Arrows, Cords, and Cadillacs. More section or curve was becoming evident in the body sides, while running boards were slowly melting into the bodies when their usefulness disappeared as cars got lower. Designers attempted to tie the car together as a whole, to integrate components such as the grille, fenders, and trunk, as opposed to designing them separately. As the 1930s neared their end, the overly

▷ The streamline era is starting to show its effects on automobile styling, as witnessed by this 1937 Cord convertible. Some consider this the most beautiful car ever produced. Pontoon fenders are starting to integrate to the body, which itself has absorbed the radiator shell and trunk. This car has no running boards, contrary to common practice with mass-produced cars until the 1940s.

organic, voluptuous shapes were slowly sprouting creases and becoming flatter, blending and melting shapes and components into one another. Headlights, tail-lights, and windows were becoming part of the body surface.

World War II had the twofold effect of cutting off Europe and its influence on American design and shifting everyone's focus to the war effort itself. Car production ceased from 1942 to 1946. When it resumed, manufacturers were selling pre-war designs for a couple of years until they could gear up for something new. That something was a more "monocoque" or "soap bar" look, heavily influenced by wartime aircraft. As the 1950s approached, limited ornamentation, combined with a lowering of the beltline and tying the headlights and taillights to that line, created a square-shouldered, clean-and-lean look. Europe was also influencing American car design again. Low-and-flashy sports cars were all the rage in Europe, and American designers were anxious to apply that style to the more-accepted larger cars built in the United States.

By the mid-1950s, car design got crazy. Exhibiting all the exuberance and opti-mism extant in America after the war, large, sculpted, be-finned behemoths prowled America's highways. Whenever possible, elements were used in a car's design to give it exaggerated and enlarged character and identity. It was a wild and wacky time for automobile styling that, in retrospect, looks playful and flamboyant compared to today's cookie-cutter, rigidly designed cars. Sure, they were excessive, but they rep-resent a time in our past that was full of energy and optimism, and they reflected it in fashion and industrial design, automobiles included. Cars were becoming much more of a personal statement and far less a mere appliance. The buzz words of 1950s car design? Lowness. Entertaining. More chrome. More glass. More overhang. More width. More... everything!

As the fashion pendulum seems to swing in extremes, cars were subdued in the 1960s (unlike some of the psychedelic-oriented and psychedelic-induced designs of that time), with safety, emissions, and government regulations becoming factors in car design. Designers were combining hard edges with a more-sculptured overall shape in an attempt to distance themselves from the extremely sculptured and finned designs that so clearly

▽ Styling had become a major selling point by the time this 1942 Chevrolet Fleetline was produced. This car also represents the last of the American cars produced until after World War II. The black, "aeroback," accessory-laden example even sports an early version of air conditioning, seen hanging from the passenger window. The chrome trim was angled just right by GM's designers to catch people's eyes in sunlight.

◁ The "soap bar" look is no more apparent than on this 1953 Hudson sedan. Introduced in 1948, Hudsons were the first mass-produced car to feature unit or "unibody" construction. The floorpan was dropped between the siderails so that it was lower than the door sills. This allowed for a lower car overall and added fuel to the longer-lower-wider revolution of the 1950s.

marked the 1950s. Classically proportioned "pony cars" with their long hoods and short decks were making the car scene starting in the mid-1960s, as was an emphasis to integrate the body and top C-pillar into one continuous surface.

The exploding popularity of the Volkswagen Beetle launched a revolution toward a more utilitarian approach to car design and packaging. The demand for economical, well-built cars like the Beetle and those products coming from Japan caught Detroit off guard. Its effects are still felt in American automobile manufacturing today. Car design was headed toward a flatter, slab-sided type of body development, reaching its zenith with the Giorgetto Giugiaro-designed Volkswagen Rabbit in the mid-1970s. By the end of that decade, car designers were hiding bumpers behind flexible bodywork for a continuous envelope from front to back, and chrome had virtually disappeared from the automotive scene.

Two events heralded car design in the 1980s: the 1982 Audi 5000 and the 1986 Ford Taurus. Both cars exhibited more rounded or organic styling combined with flush glass. With an easing of U.S. federal regulations, both cars used flush headlights that conformed to the body. Though criticized by rivals as a "jellybean" design, the impact of these two designs will be felt through the end of the century. Most car companies have developed new shapes, with even more-extreme organic designs entering the marketplace. Some designs from Chrysler have ushered in the cab-forward proportions as the design wave of the future—which leads us up to today.

Some would say that the surge in popularity of sport-utility vehicles and pickups is a reaction to the current crop of domestic and imported "cookie-cutter" cars. Others believe that we are approaching a period much like the mid-1950s, where organic and sheer designs will converge, resulting in a more playful approach to design.

Wherever automotive design is headed, there is that inexplicable attraction that leads many to view cars as high art and prompts us to want to get involved in their design by drawing them. And this is where we begin.

△ This 1956 Chevrolet "Sport Sedan" represents the middle year of the 1955-1956-1957 triumvirate from Chevrolet. Styling by the mid-1950s was taking a dramatic turn toward more exciting exercises after the conservative period immediately after the War. With such flamboyant features as tri-tone paint jobs, reversible seat cushions, and lots of chrome, the 1950s were bringing consumers more than they could have ever imagined. Vestiges of "fins" were showing up on all makes, with 1957 officially starting the who-can-produce-the-tallest-fins race.

▷ The 1959 Cadillac is the quintessential finned 1950s car, represented by Larry Watson's mildly customized coupe. In most cases, by 1961 the fins were gone, showing how critical styling and change had become in the auto industry. New designs were being introduced yearly to the delight of jaded car-crazy consumers tired of previous years' models.

△ By 1961 most of the fins got snipped, though in an odd twist some makes sprouted smaller fins on their lower quarters. An example of the combined severity of both of these interesting features can be seen on this 1961 Oldsmobile. Styling was becoming a bit more refined, with the long-hood, short-deck proportions ushered in by the "pony car" stampede-leading 1964½ Mustang.

▽ Though not representative of the car most people drive, this Viper convertible is indicative of the return to more organic shapes witnessed through most of the 1990s and into the next century. As the pendulum for automotive design tends to swing in extremes, don't be surprised if the car companies start moving away from this look in the near future.

Tools and Equipment

If you own pencils and paper, then you have the basics to draw anything. Right? Actually, there are many tricks that will help make your drawings and sketches easier to do, look more professional, and help you do them in less time. One trick is to have a comfortable, well-lit work area and equipment that will enhance your ability and desire to draw cars. Be forewarned: Having this equipment without knowing drawing basics won't help you a bit, just as the best bat, glove, and uniform do not make for the next Mike Piazza. This analogy holds true for computers, too, but more on that in Chapter 15. All this equipment is an aid, but not a replacement, for your drawing abilities.

First off, you need a good drawing surface on which to work. A solid table, desk, drafting or light table is the preferred choice. Whatever your decision, the key word is sturdy. Don't settle for one of those wobbly, bottom-of-the-line drafting tables with the hinge-and-catch brackets that have been known to amputate whole arms and hands (just kidding). Make sure its left edge is straight and square so you can run a T-square along this edge for the occasional need to square things up on your drawings. If you need a surface that tilts, a drafting table is your best bet.

Whatever drawing surface you work on, having good lighting is best, for obvious reasons. I like incandescent lighting, but you may wish to combine fluorescent and incandescent lights, or prefer working under fluorescent conditions exclusively. Lighting should be even to

▷ There are so many choices when it comes to drawing utensils that you'll never know what they all do. Different pencils and pens yield different looks to a drawing, so it comes down to how comfortable they feel, the type of line they create, and their performance in terms of drying, consistency, flow, and endurance. The good part is that they're usually cheap, so experiment with as many as you like!

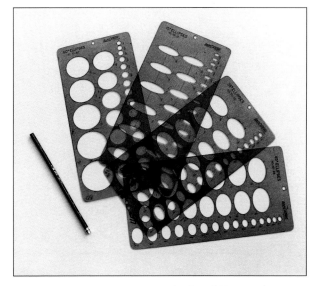

△ Once you decide to pick a brand of marker, a good range of colors is important. In terms of your health and the environment, alcohol-based markers are better than the chemical-based ones. This is just one of three banks of markers I use to give myself the widest range possible.

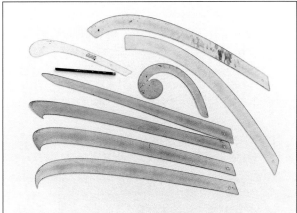

△ Sets of ellipse templates are available in 10-degree to 80-degree ranges. These sets come in small and large sizes. Start with the smaller set (shown) first, then see where your needs take you.

◁ To draw cars, you might think an artist would need the most contorted and animated set of sweeps available. It's just the opposite. The almost straight sweep in the middle of this picture is the one I use the most. Since I made these particular sweeps and they are not available commercially, try to find close duplicates.

avoid shadows or hot spots, so more than one light source will probably work best to spread out the light. I have three lamps at my drawing board. An articulating light is best for the occasional need to zone-in for close-up work. Let's face it—you have to be able to see what you are doing, so start with a well-lit work space.

As for your implement of choice, try experimenting with different types of pens and pencils until you find the one with which you are most comfortable. I based my choice of Verithin 747 black pencils on the fact that they smear less, put down a nice black line, and don't break as easily as a lead pencil (I guess I have a heavy hand). Also, I find I have a bit more control with them; they tend to put out more resistance so my freehand line doesn't blast out of control over the paper. You may prefer the qualities that a No. 2 lead pencil offers, or a fine-tip pen, or even a ballpoint pen. I know people who sketch with all of them, and they can all produce nice, "juicy" sketches.

If you use any type of wood pencil, you must have an electric pencil sharpener. Taking the time to sharpen a dull pencil after a few strokes is as annoying as an oil-down after each round of drag racing. And in such a circumstance, you are more likely to run with a dull pencil, which will produce a marginal sketch at best. Why do you think they call them dull? Step up and get the electric sharpener so that you can flog away.

Once you start to tighten up your sketches, you'll want to look into templates and angles to help guide you and your pencil. 45-degree and 30/60-degree angles come in a variety of sizes, so take your best shot. One of each will work just fine.

△ Keep a can of Bestine handy for cleaning dirty sweeps and other instruments you gunk up with marker juice and pencil lead. It can also be used to create interesting backgrounds depicted in the rendering sequence later in this book. A spray bomb of fixative works well for keeping pencil or chalk down on your drawing, reducing the instance of smudging. However, it allows you to come back into a sketch and work these sprayed areas later on.

Although the colored variety of angles looks cooler, stick with the clear ones, as it's easier to see your work through them.

Templates consist not only of the circle and ellipse variety, but will also include French curves, or "sweeps." The ellipse templates come in sets ranging from 10 to 80 degrees; 100 degrees is a full circle. Sizes within the range go from ¼ to 2 inches in the smaller template set. Start with this smaller set first and see if you have any need for the larger set, as they can be a bit pricey. These larger ellipse sets range in size from a 2- to 4-inch ellipse. They are great for larger drawings, but you may find you are more comfortable drawing smaller, in which case you won't need the larger set at all.

As for French curves and sweeps, they will help in tuning up a line. They should not be used as a replacement for freehand drawing, but as an enhancement. Most art stores carry a range of configurations from which to choose. Though the more complex and irregular curves look intriguing, try to find curves that display slight bows and gentle curves. These adapt better to car illustrations than the crazy-curve variety of French curve. I made the sweeps I use as a school project many moons ago. You can't buy them, though I've seen similar examples from time to time. They are about 20 inches and work perfectly for car illustration and design. Check out the photos and see if you can find something that looks similar at your local art store.

Templates and T-squares get dirty. A good solvent or thinner like Bestine dumped on some tissue works great for cleaning up your smudged and dirty equipment. Do it often while you are in the middle of a drawing. Nothing looks worse than a smeared and dirty drawing caused by filthy hands and equipment. Don't be lazy— keep those hands and tools clean!

Other small but necessary items to have on hand are a variety of erasers. I prefer the Pink Pearl and white vinyl type in pencil form. Since you probably will have a specific area you wish to erase, these thinner erasers get in that small area and do the job. The larger Pink Pearl and kneaded gray erasers take no prisoners. When you erase, they go for it all. Not good! Stick with those slender ones. Some have a peel-back outer skin, while others insert into a plastic holder. The other advantage is that you may want to use a controlled erasure to create a highlight (more on this in Chapter 10). Slicing off the end gives you an incredibly sharp edge to erase with, which leads to a crisp erasure. To get that clean slice you will need to purchase

△ You'll not only erase with one of these pencil-type erasers, you'll also create highlights and reflections by removing drawn or rendered material in the illustration. This is also demonstrated in the rendering sequence.

▽ An X-ACTO knife is a "must-have" item for the budding artist. Different blades give you different types of control.

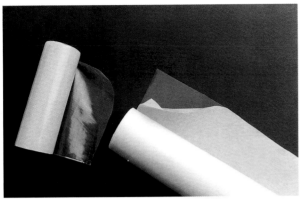

an X-ACTO knife. These razor-sharp knives have myriad uses, from cutting eraser ends and matte board to scraping dirt spots off negatives and film positives. Just be careful. They slice through skin as if it were butter!

Masking tape also comes in handy, but I prefer drafting tape. It sticks less so you can get it off your paper or board without destroying your latest creation. But there is also another reason. Some artists use the stuff to mask off an area of the drawing much as you might use frisket or masking film. What's frisket? It is a brand of thin vinyl film with an adhesive backing that you cut to a specific shape to protect or isolate an area on which you are working. Some artists use it to mask off the paper around the image they're drawing to keep it clean from fingerprints and sweaty hands. In Chapter 10 I'll show you how to use Nitto tape, which is similar to frisket without the peel-off backing. Since masking film can be a bit expensive, you may want to practice with the drafting tape first. Then, as you feel the need to be a bit more discriminating, you can try out the variety of film available.

Finally, you'll need something on which to draw. Zillions of paper types and illustration boards are available to suit every desire. Start with a couple of different bond paper tablets at least 9x12 inches or larger. You will find that paper varies in texture, thickness, and shades of white. Some take pencils better; some take markers or chalks better. You'll need to experiment to see which type best fits your particular requirements. As we get into the actual drawing portions of this book, I will suggest certain types of paper or board that work well for those applications being discussed. But the real joy in drawing is to tailor your choices to what works best for you.

△ Masking film is demonstrated in the rendering sequence—here are two choices. Nitto tape, left, has no backing. You just unroll the amount you wish to use and slap it down. Frisket film is on the right. Primarily used by airbrush artists, it has a peel-off backing and is available in roll or sheet form, in a matte or glossy finish.

△ Reference material in the form of photos, clippings, magazines, and books is essential to expand your knowledge of automobiles and your visual library. In most cases, this reference is a rich source for determining reflections, color, shadow, and light. It also can become a base for going beyond reality once you start experimenting with rendering your car sketches.

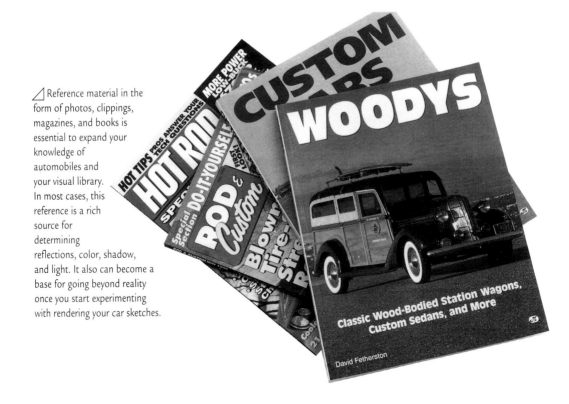

Perspective

Beginners cringe at the thought of perspective, but you have to admit it's very cool once you see that car sitting on your paper like it was a real 3-D object! You don't want to be drawing side views all your life, so get through this chapter and apply what you have learned to your next car drawing. You've heard it before: You'll improve with practice.

There is a mechanical way to draw in perspective, but it is a methodical process that does not allow for exaggeration or emphasis. Simple steps are covered in this chapter, but the best advice is to look with your eyes and brain, to visualize what it is you wish to draw. Relying on methods and plotting slows the drawing process and does not make for a fun drawing experience.

To begin, you must make some decisions. The first is to select which view of the car you would like to see. This will determine how much of the front, side, or back

When placing an as-yet-to-be-drawn object on a flat plane, the horizon line will dictate the view or eye level of your object. An artist represents linear perspective by pointing all the lines in his imaginary space toward a vanishing point. The borders represent the limits to the space we are creating within, and the rising sun represents the beginning of your journey to draw cars properly. Good luck!

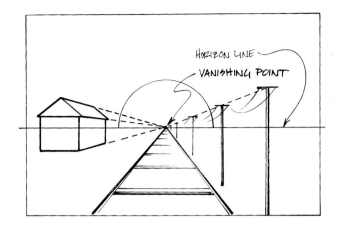

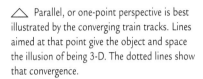

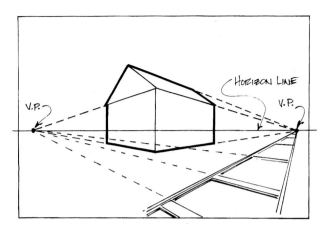

△ Parallel, or one-point perspective is best illustrated by the converging train tracks. Lines aimed at that point give the object and space the illusion of being 3-D. The dotted lines show that convergence.

△ Lines that vanish in two directions illustrate angular or two-point perspective. This is a truer simulation of reality than the one-point perspective example, and is the setup for virtually all car depictions. As objects go back into our space, they foreshorten. This means they shorten up because we actually see less as their sides angle away from us.

▽ Moving the horizon line to the upper portions of the space we have created yields a higher view than the previous example, which put the eye level right at the horizon line. This is a good perspective to illustrate an interesting feature on the hood or top of a car. It also allows you to see into the windshield.

of the car you wish to show. Usually, what is known as a "front 3/4 view" is the most common angle chosen to draw cars because it tends to give the best sense of what the car looks like. Next, you must choose the viewer's angle. Do you want to look down on the vehicle, as if from a tall vantage point, or see it much like you would if you were walking along a street? Or right at it, as if you were on your hands and knees? Or from a worm's-eye view, or what is called a ground-level view? This will determine the horizon line and vanishing points.

The horizon line is that point out in the distance where the sky and ground meet. Hypothetically, if it is a clear day and you are looking across an uninterrupted stretch of desert or field, it is the line in the distance at which the sky meets the field, or desert floor. Obviously, the horizon line is rarely seen in real life because it is usually covered up by buildings, trees, walls—you name it. Yet, if you are to construct an accurate drawing of a car, and/or its surroundings, you need to draw or at least visualize this line. It is usually placed in the middle of a page but its location determines how the car is viewed. A low horizon line will result in a view looking down, a high

▽ A low horizon line gives you a low or worm's-eye view of the object. With the vanishing points within the space we have created, it gives the object a very forced or extreme look.

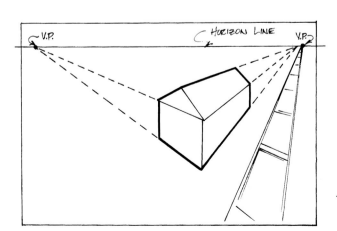

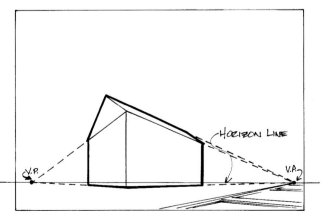

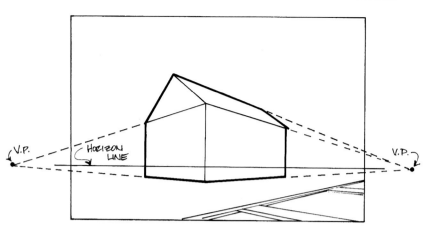

A better solution may be placing the vanishing points outside the borders of our space. This gives a more realistic view of the object. You may want to practice placement of both the horizon line and vanishing points to see some of the different setups possible.

horizon line will give you a worm's-eye view of the subject, and in between will give you variations of these two extremes.

The vanishing point is that point at which the lines of a diminishing object disappear at the horizon line. But this description is a lot more confusing to understand than the simple example of the train tracks. The vanishing point for train tracks is that point at which the tracks come together out in the distance at the horizon line.

There are really only two types of vanishing point setups. The first is the single-point perspective, where only one vanishing point is used. The railroad track scenario fits this example best. Next is the two-point perspective, which is the usual method used to draw a car. Rather than describe it here, the accompanying examples will help you better understand the two-point perspective and how it relates to drawing cars.

Objects in perspective lose detail and value as they go back into the atmosphere of the imaginary space you have created in your sketch. Atmosphere softens the details and lightens the values. To visually pull an object toward you, adding more detail and value are two of several things you can do to trick the eye. This works in the artist's favor, as it becomes unnecessary to put as much effort into the detail of objects farther back in perspective.

I talk about value here and throughout the book. Value refers to the lightness or darkness an object exhibits either in color or in black and white. Pastel colors, yellow, and definitely white have light values. Orange, most reds, greens, and blues fall into the medium value category. Purple and the darker blues, reds, greens, browns, and especially black all exhibit a darker value.

We assign numbers for values in a gray value scale from 1 to 10, with 1 being the lightest value and 10 being the darkest. You can see how value is assigned to a car rendering in Chapters 7 and 8.

Just to finish off our perspective lesson, there is such a thing as three-point perspective. It is a trick artists use when trying to give an object the sense of being very large. This usually does not apply to drawing cars, although you might want to see hints of it in Chapter 12.

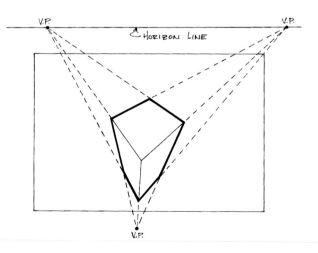

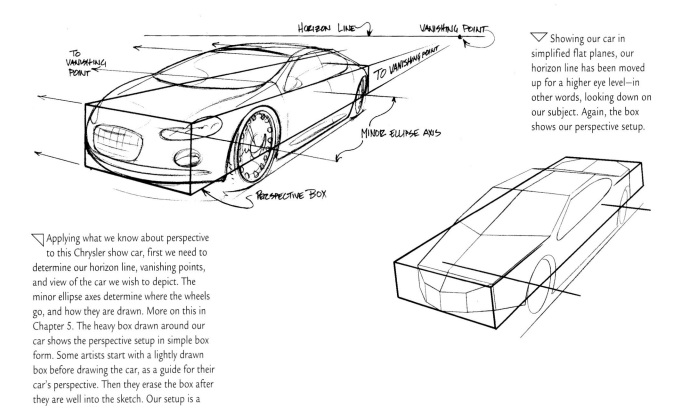

▽ Showing our car in simplified flat planes, our horizon line has been moved up for a higher eye level—in other words, looking down on our subject. Again, the box shows our perspective setup.

▽ Applying what we know about perspective to this Chrysler show car, first we need to determine our horizon line, vanishing points, and view of the car we wish to depict. The minor ellipse axes determine where the wheels go, and how they are drawn. More on this in Chapter 5. The heavy box drawn around our car shows the perspective setup in simple box form. Some artists start with a lightly drawn box before drawing the car, as a guide for their car's perspective. Then they erase the box after they are well into the sketch. Our setup is a typical front view of a car.

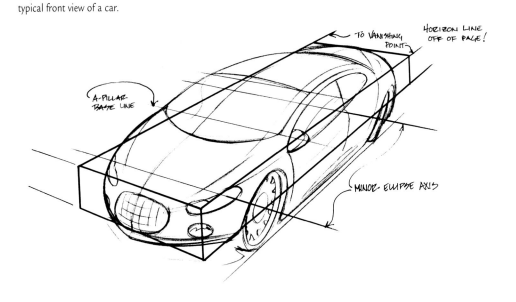

◁ With the planed surfaces smoothed out to represent a real car, you can see the shape take place, and how the view is from a different vantage point, or eye level, from the previous view. Organic cars like this one are a bit harder to draw. If you are having some problems, you might choose a flatter, more angular car to practice this with.

◿ Our subject Chrysler show car shown in yet another eye level. This time, our vantage point is almost at the ground, for a worm's-eye view. Indicating the box around the subject in this view would be confusing, so it has been left out. But the arrows show where our perspective lines are converging—which is waaaay out beyond this book. The view makes for a very powerful, dramatic setup for your drawing.

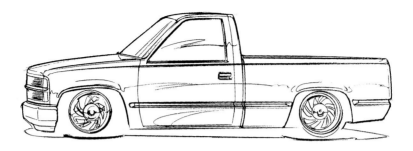

△ This truck side view gives us a starting point for determining details before we spin it into perspective. Again, at this point we will need to choose where to place the horizon line, to give us our eye level, as well as which view of the truck we want to show.

◁ The simple box drawing shows the view and the basic perspective setup. The cartoon gives the eye level, which places the horizon line a little above the middle of the space we have created.

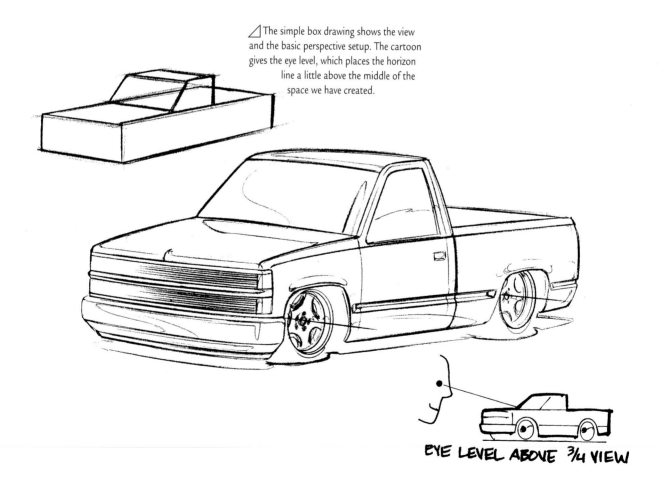

EYE LEVEL ABOVE ¾ VIEW

A low horizon line gives a ground or low eye level. The box drawing shows the perspective lines being almost parallel. This happens when our eye level is in the middle of an object, as shown in the cartoon. With the perspective lines being parallel, this becomes the simplest perspective to create.

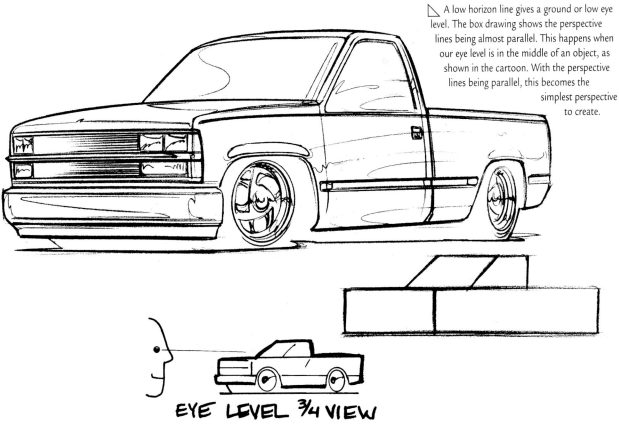

EYE LEVEL ¾ VIEW

With a high horizon line, we look down on the truck. The sides of the truck foreshorten, which means that due to our extreme eye level, the sides get shorter to our eye. Also because of the eye level, the ellipses we use to create the tires and wheels are tighter. See Chapter 5 for more on circles and round objects in perspective.

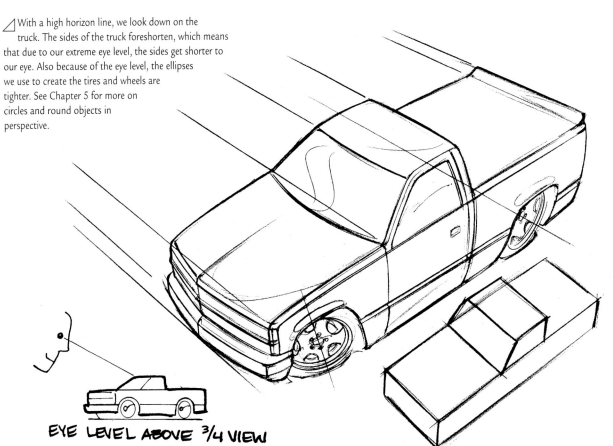

EYE LEVEL ABOVE ¾ VIEW

◿ A finished sketch with a high horizon-line location. Since vans can be a bit boring drawn from a normal perspective, I did this set-up for a bit of drama, and to show off the spoiler created for this real-life project.

Proportion

You may have heard the term "proportion" bandied about when describing that latest mouth-watering creation from Car Land and wondered just what it meant. Proportion refers to the relationship of the visual elements that make up the car to one another. We're talking about the side windows, their size, and how they relate to the body; how the size and height of the body relates to the top or wheelbase; or how the overhang at the front or rear of the car looks in relation to the body, the top, or the wheelbase. The result of the relationships of these visual elements gives the car a pleasing balance or feel. The "feel" of a car can be a very subjective thing, which is why you see so many different types of automobiles on the road, from vans to sports cars to sedans and trucks. This is also the reason, within each of these categories, we see so many variations in design and proportion.

▷ The building blocks for proportion are the simple one-, two-, and three-box groups. Keeping these in mind should aid you in visualizing a car's proportions or as a loose guideline on paper. One-box proportions include vans and even 1920s and 1930s roadsters and tourings.

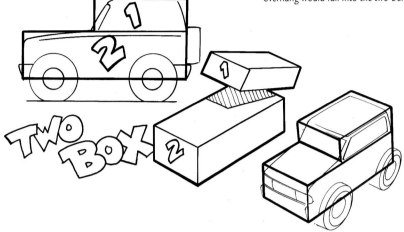

Vehicles with two-box proportions include sport utility vehicles, station wagons, hatchbacks, and fastbacks. Also, any van with an extreme amount of front overhang would fall into the two-box category.

Proportions can also be slotted into three general categories, known as one-box, two-box, and three-box design. One-box design is made up of vans without any front engine overhang or crush zone, and I suppose you could include 1920s and 1930s roadsters here, too. Two-box design includes vans with a front overhang, station wagons, sport-utilities like Range Rovers and Blazers, hatchbacks, and fastbacks like those cool "aeroback" GM fastbacks from the late 1940s. Three-box designs are mostly sedans, hardtops, and pick-up trucks.

Paying attention to the proportions of the car you are drawing can partially determine whether it looks right or wrong. One of the easiest ways to ascertain whether you are on the mark in terms of proportion is to scale the car to an element of itself.

Huh?

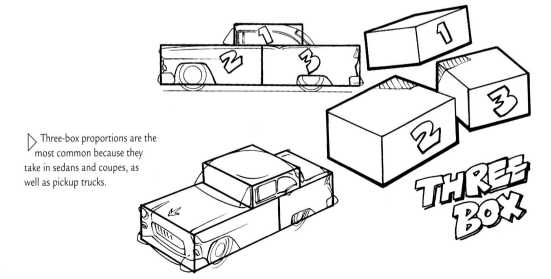

Three-box proportions are the most common because they take in sedans and coupes, as well as pickup trucks.

Well, you know that tires are mostly in the 25- to 27-inch range. You can use this as a means to scale your drawing. In other words, to measure dimensions roughly. We're not talking about an accurately scaled diagram, just a quick-and-easy way to see if you are in the range of acceptability with the proportions you have chosen to draw. It's an aid that is both fun and easy.

An example: The height might be three tires high, the wheelbase five tires long, and front and rear overhang one tire each. Armed with this information, you now have an aid to spin that car into perspective and have it turn out in proportion. Of course, proportion is another common problem seen in drawings that are not done properly, whether by an amateur or professional. Exaggerating proportion is also one of the first things relied upon to turn a drawing into a cartoon.

Another method is a grid system based on a side view of the car. Not as methodical as perspective plotting, it is a helpful guide in giving your drawing a 3-D look. Draw a box around your car's side view and grid it off in some convenient division. Then draw the box and grid lightly on your paper, in perspective. Since you should be able to place a box in perspective, this method allows you to use the grid within the box as your guide. Until you get comfortable with your "visualization" of the car you wish to draw, you may want to use this method as a means to get those proportions right.

◹ Here's a good trick to help you. Wheelbase is very important when determining the proportions of any vehicle. Using an element of the car you are drawing for scale, like a tire, can be a terrific aid in figuring out the wheelbase and can help you with its proportions. A general rule of thumb would be 3 tires for regular cars and trucks, 2½ for smaller cars like a Honda hatchback, and 3½ or more for larger cars and limousines.

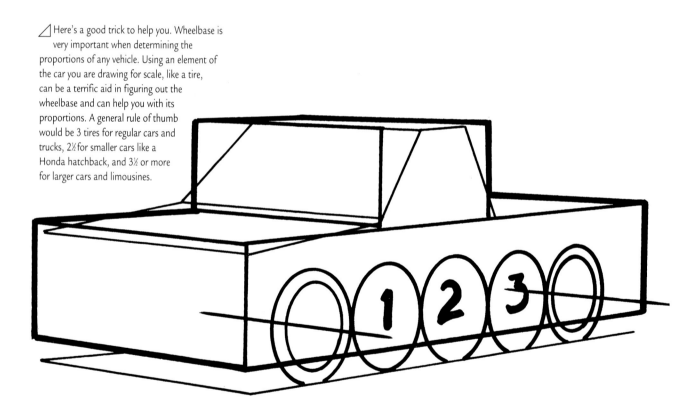

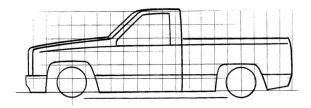

△ Transferring the grid to perspective requires you to foreshorten the grid. Follow where the side view lines fall in the grid and you now have a semblance of the side in perspective. Now, roughly build out from the side toward the vanishing point to create your front end, hood, windshield, and the rest of the truck.

△ Gridding can sometimes be of help if you start with a side view. However, I find that this method takes a lot of time for what you end up with. I'll demonstrate it, but be forewarned that I don't consider it the best for determining a car's proportions in perspective. Once your side view is determined, draw a convenient grid over it.

△ Use your rough perspective as an underlay, or erase the grid, and finish off the drawing. As you can see, we have a fairly good representation of a late-model truck. If used as a crutch for a short time to elevate your awareness of proportion and perspective, then it is a good method to try.

△ It would be hard to achieve a drawing like this with the grid method, which is why I use it to make a point. This drawing was achieved by studying photographs and roughing out the proportions freehand. It took a couple of overlays before I had it in a form from which I could do a finished drawing. As you can see, visualizing, good freehand sketching, understanding proportion, and some time have given us a better truck drawing.

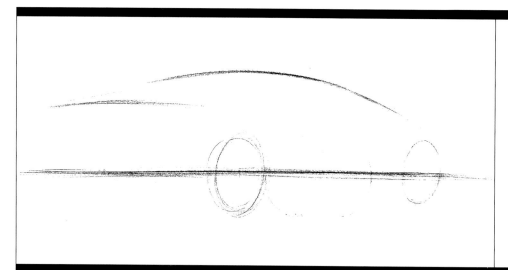

◁ If we can jump ahead just a bit with some sketching methods from Chapter 6, plus what you know about perspective and proportioning, there is an easier way to sketch out a car. This is an especially good trick when your eye level is in line with the side of the car so that your perspective lines are almost parallel. Start with a line that represents the minor axis of the wheels, and also gives you a guide for determining the three-tire proportions. Loosely rough out a silhouette or outline of the car you wish to sketch.

▷ Sketch in the bottom or rockers, as well as a front and back. I draw these lines in very lightly at first, then darken or tighten them up as I "feel" the car taking shape. We now have an outline of the car, which we will soon fill in with more details.

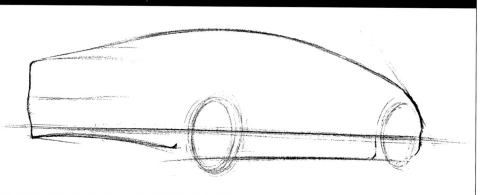

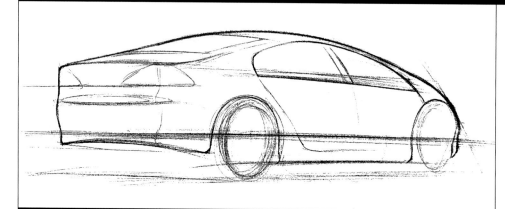

◁ Window lines, taillights, door cuts, and miscellaneous details start to give our sedan some life.

▷ Reflection and wheel design guidelines, as well as ground shadow, sets us up for the final details.

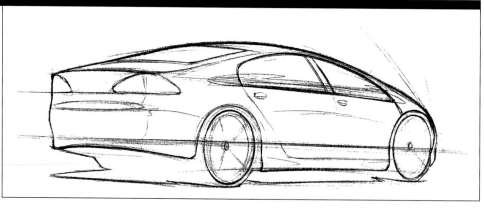

◿ Our finished sketch is a result of some
perspective and proportion tricks, and also
"feeling" the sketch as we go.

Ellipses and Axes

Placing round or cylindrical objects in perspective is the most common mistake I see in drawings and illustrations, yet it is the simplest theory in practice. I guess they did not cover it in some art schools, or those without a firm grasp of the concept may not have bothered to analyze how to put a cylindrical object properly into perspective.

This is yet another easy method to pick up. Quite simply, an ellipse is just a circle in perspective. As you will see in the examples, the keys to putting a tire or steering wheel or any round object into perspective are the major and minor axes of the ellipse. That, and an intelligent eye, should work every time. The one point to remember is that there are no points on a cylindrical object in perspective except on a football! A tin can, bowl, or tire laying on its side—none of these objects have pointy ends.

With this in mind, refer to the drawings in this chapter for simple methods and aids to help you nail down this final technical portion of drawing, before we move on to some less-technical aspects of drawing cars.

▷ Since it is easy for us to put a box into perspective, this is how we will begin to help us place circular objects, like tires, wheels, and headlights into perspective. The dot represents the center of the box in the first example, and the perspective center of the box in the second example. When the circle is placed into perspective, it becomes an ellipse. Notice that the ellipse is a continuous curve and that there are no points at the tight ends of the ellipse.

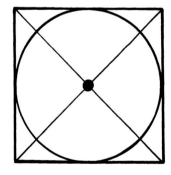

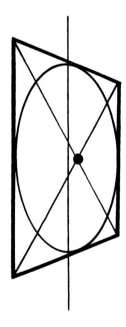

Eliminating the box, we have a circle with its center represented by the cross lines. Flipping the circle into perspective gives us a better relationship of the cross lines, known as the major and minor axes. For car illustration, we will be most concerned with the minor axis, as this represents the axle or centerline, which is always used as a guide to determine whether our wheels are in perspective.

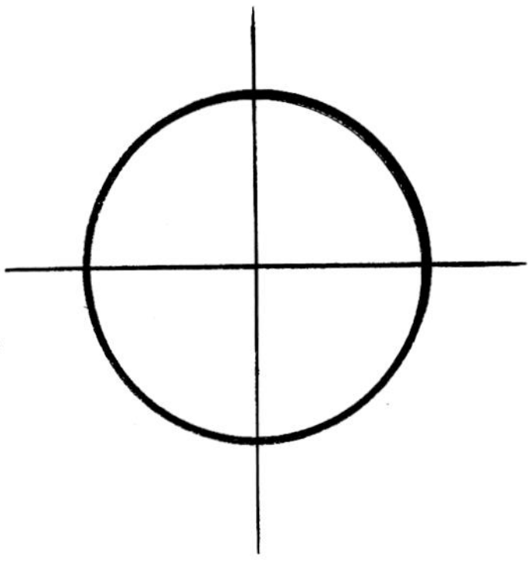

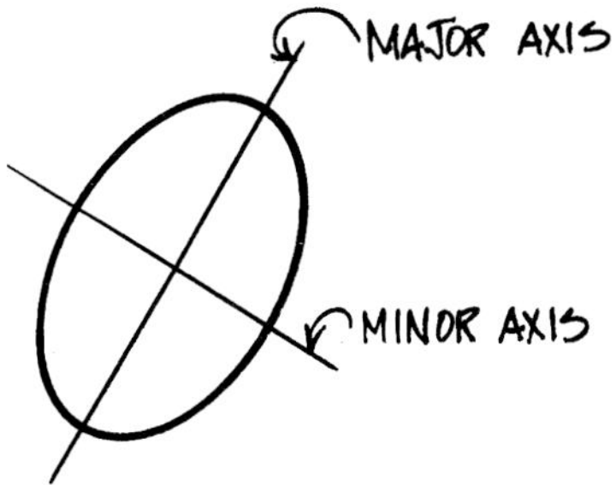

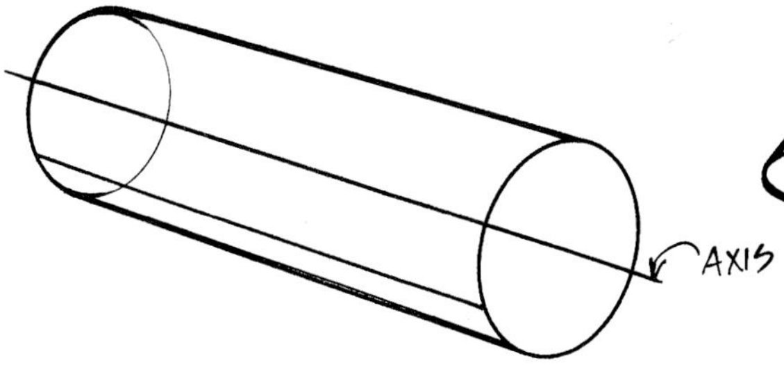

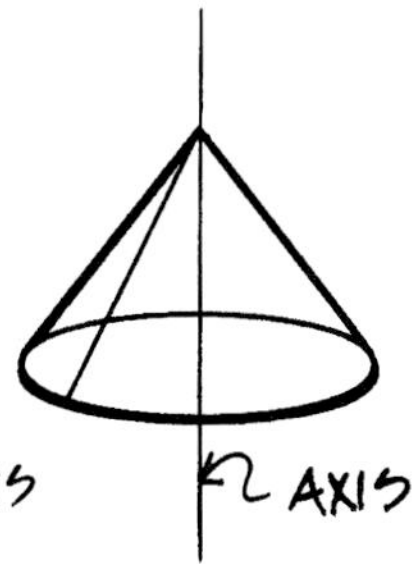

Creating a cylinder or cone relies on the minor axis. In the cone's case, its point rests somewhere on the minor axis, depending on how tall you would like to make it. For our cylinder, the minor axis determines its far end or end cut. Since the cylinder is going back into perspective, we know to converge our sides slightly, which means our far-end ellipse will be slightly smaller than the front one.

Again, the minor axis is the guide from which we create a cocktail glass. Notice how the bottom ellipse is less pinched than the top one. This is because as we move down, away from the horizon line, we see more of the glass.

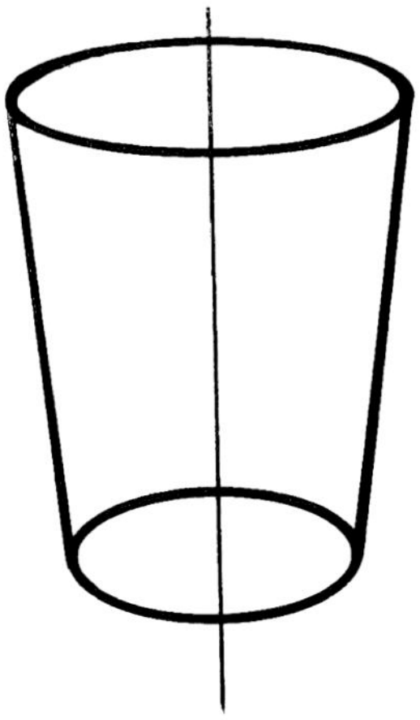

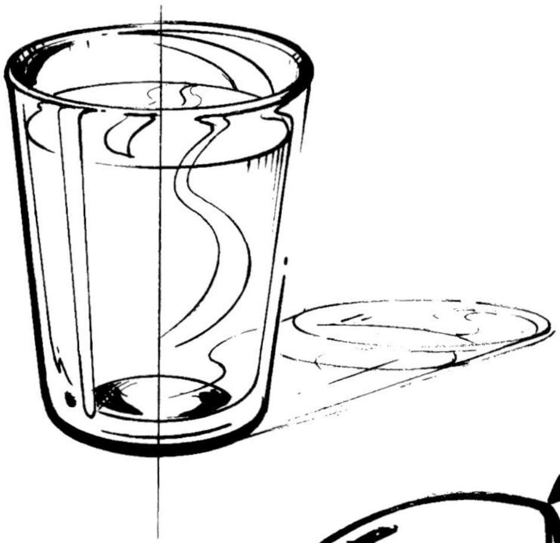

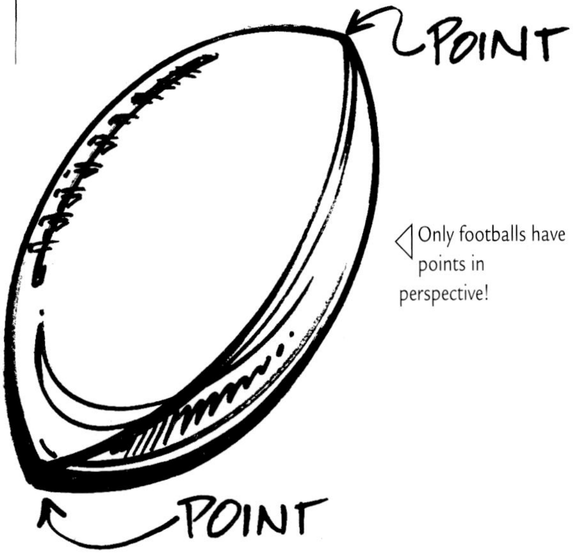

Only footballs have points in perspective!

◺ Ellipses are identified by degrees, with the tightest being almost 0 degrees and a full circle being 100 degrees. As mentioned with the cocktail glass, as circular objects move away from the horizon line, their degree of roundness becomes larger. A circle sitting on the horizon line becomes a line itself, or 0 degrees, while moving above or below the horizon line yields a larger-degree ellipse the further you go.

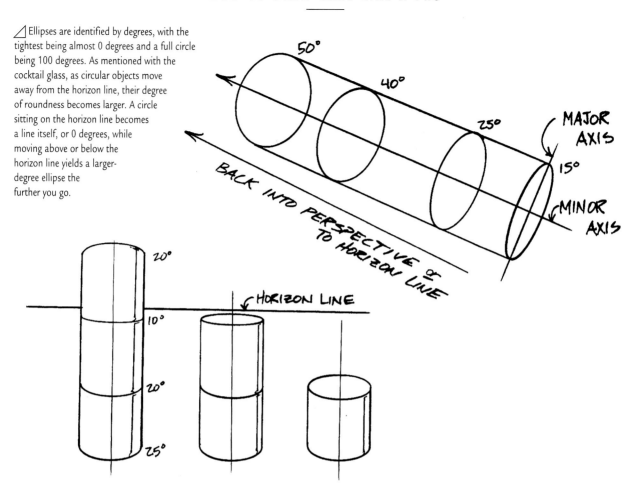

▽ A combination wheel/tire assembly is just a series of built-up ellipses. The vanishing points will dictate the angle that the tire tread face takes. Because the axis is representing the center of the car's axle, it becomes the predominant concern when constructing a tire/wheel combination for your car drawing.

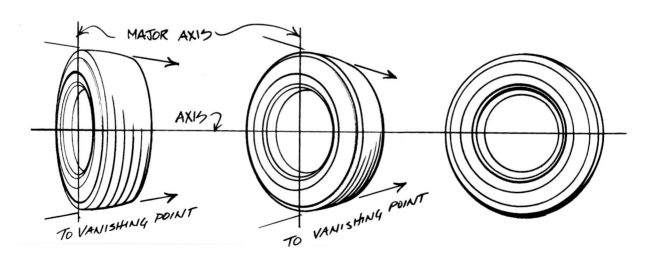

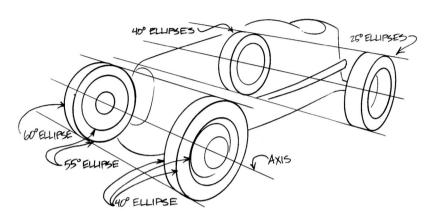

This open-wheeled Lakester from the 1940s gives us a chance to see how the tire/wheel assembly is set up in perspective. With the minor axis pointing to the left vanishing point, notice how the ellipses get smaller as they move closer to the horizon line. Moving toward the left vanishing point, our ellipses are less pinched. But moving toward the right vanishing point, we see less of the face of the tire and more of the tread. If we used the same ellipse for our two front wheels, it would give the illusion that the car was steering into itself— not good!

Sketching and Line Quality

Sketching techniques are as varied as signatures, and in many ways are like a signature. The way a drawing is sketched can define who did the work by the particular technique and the artist's style. I'll get into the different types of drawing tools and how they can change an artist's style in another chapter. Here, I'll develop some basic suggestions to try out. The ability to sketch should come easily, so some of these suggestions may be too cumbersome for your own taste. Not to worry. Use what you can from this chapter, or try to adapt some of these suggestions to your own style of drawing.

The main objective is to have fun and stay loose when you draw and sketch. A relaxed and free hand, drawing from your whole arm—even your whole body—instead of quick rips from the wrist, helps you maintain a nice flow to your drawings and results in more controllable lines. You've seen the "chicken scratch" style of drawing with short, quick strokes and jabs. My observations and practice of drawing styles have shown me that this style can be very distracting and less professional. You may want to pay particular attention to the way lines are delineated and also their weights and emphasis.

Line weights are the thick and thin lines you see throughout a sketch. Variations in line weight hold your attention longer and are a lot more interesting to look at than lines that are consistent. From the artist's standpoint, they are also more fun to create and are probably easier and quicker to do than a drawing with repetitive line weights throughout. Typically, you give more emphasis or line weight to a line that is closer to you, a line that helps to represent an undercut edge, an edge that is defining something round, or a part of a drawing that calls for some extra pressure. After all, it's as much a tactile experience as it is a visual one. Combine these elements and you have line quality.

A great sketch contains lots of different line weights that contribute to its line quality. Don't get bogged down by common weights. Give your drawing some spark and interest by varying those weights. You can feel the difference.

Dave "Big" Deal is one of the premier cartoonists in the country. This Lotus 7 shows you why. Look at all of the varying line weights and how Deal attacks certain areas to create movement, while others are finessed to create detail. The complete range of black and white values are all there, to make for a more interesting sketch. It pulls you in to see more even if you aren't trying to learn drawing techniques. That's what makes Big Deal such a big deal!

▷ Sketching can be a blast—just ask Ed Newton. He has been drawing cars professionally for more than 30 years. Check out this video box rough for Sega Genesis. Notice the long pencil strokes, great use of thick and thin line work, and the movement he creates with the direction of his lines and exaggerated perspective.

▽ John Bell is car crazy and a mad sketch artist, but puts steak and potatoes on the table by working for the film industry. Among his many credits, Bell was co-art director for *Jurassic Park*. His ballpoint pen sketches are simple and clean but possess tons of quality with line emphasis in certain portions of the sketch, subtle reflection indication, and guidelines for himself and the viewer to help delineate surface sections.

▽ Another John Bell sketch incorporating a bit of marker and colored pencil. This freehand sketch has been tuned up with the help of a sweep or two after the initial light drawing. Notice how he started off with a simple box to keep himself in perspective. Even the pros use guides—so should you.

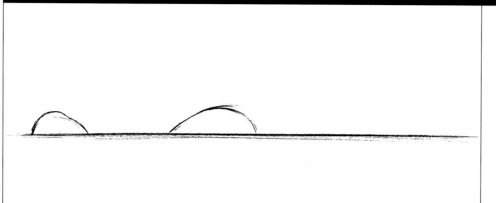

Let's try a sketch that doesn't require drawing boxes for perspective help. This sketch will put our eye level right in the middle of the car, so we don't have to be as concerned with vanishing points. Remember why? Our line represents the point from which we will build this sketch. It becomes the horizon line, approximate middle of the body, location of the minor axis, and also the point at which we'll place our headlights.

I've picked a point back from the headlights for our front wheel, and approximately 2½ tires back I have placed the second tire in a tighter ellipse. This gives me a point to determine the approximate bottom of the car and a ground line.

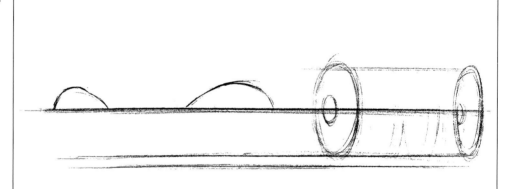

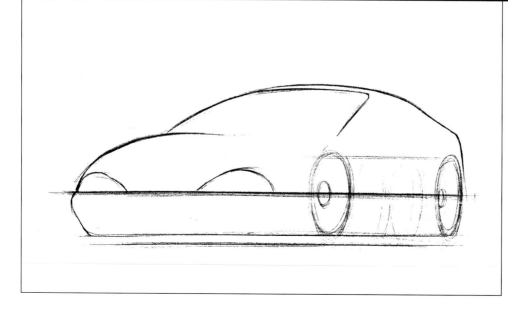

We'll rough in the outline or silhouette of the car, plus indicate the windshield A-pillar location. If you do these stages lightly at first, you can change them later if you don't like where they fall.

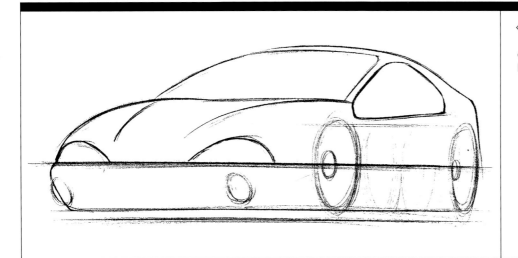

◁ A bit of hood detail, some fog lamp indication, and a side daylight opening (DLO) start to bring this sketch around.

▷ Detailing out the lamps and wheels, and a bit of reflection indication, just about completes this sketch.

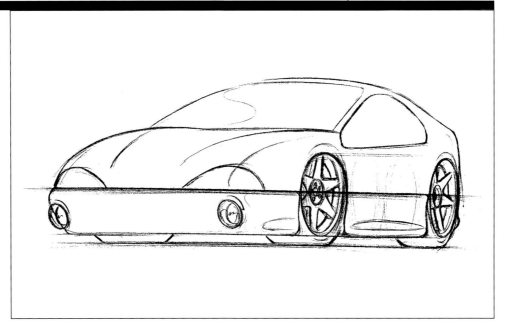

◁ A grille opening and some quick black marker complete our "hot hatch" quick sketch.

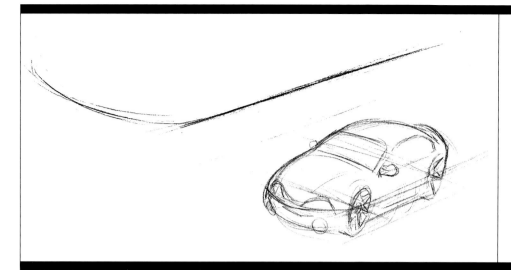

With little perspective to deal with, our first "hot hatch" sketch was almost like cheating. Now, let's put that same car into a real perspective and see what we get. To give me lines from which to build off, I did a quick and dirty perspective thumbnail. From that, I drew my wheel center guidelines.

As with the previous sketch, I use the center as a build-off point for my wheels and headlights.

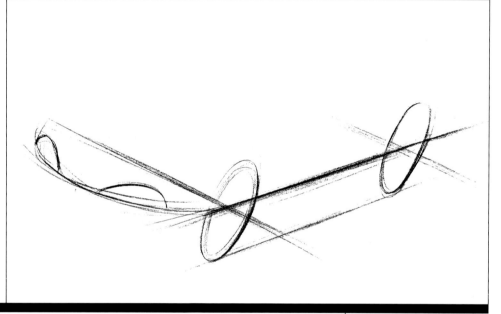

With the wheel and headlight information, I can now outline the silhouette, which gives me a build-off point for the windshield and bottom of the car. At this point you can play with proportion and silhouettes to give you anything from a truck to a race car. It's fun to experiment at this stage of the sketch.

◁ Fog lamp indication came as a natural outgrowth of determining the bottom of the car. Wheel detail and a little more fill-in starts to bring this sketch to life.

▷ More detail and some reflection and door cut indication give us an almost complete sketch.

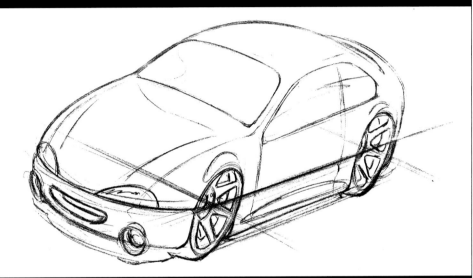

▷ This rough sketch can now be used as an underlay, or the guidelines and errant line work can be erased or cleaned up if you prefer a tighter sketch. This perspective is very descriptive for car illustration.

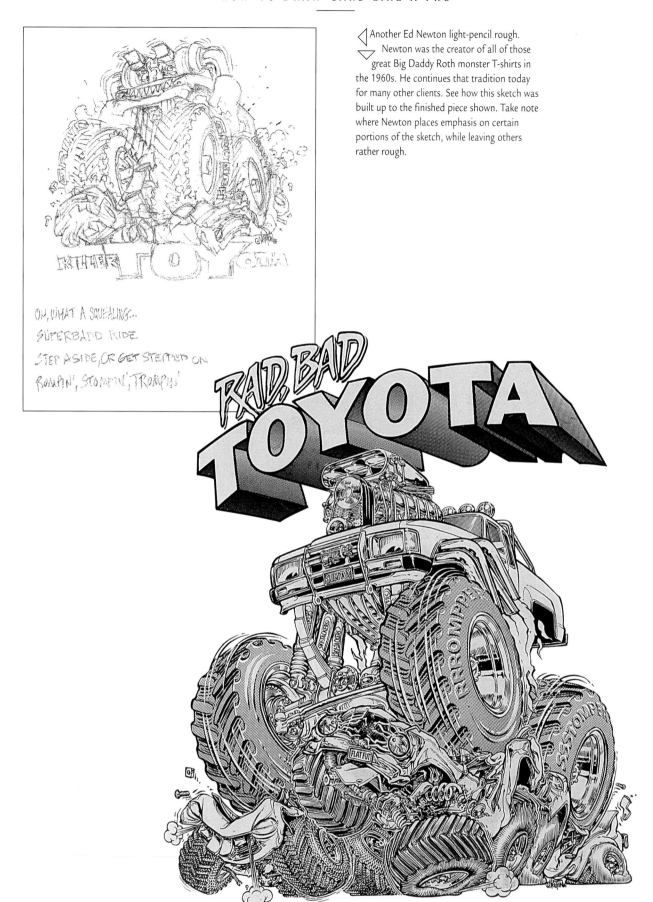

Another Ed Newton light-pencil rough. Newton was the creator of all of those great Big Daddy Roth monster T-shirts in the 1960s. He continues that tradition today for many other clients. See how this sketch was built up to the finished piece shown. Take note where Newton places emphasis on certain portions of the sketch, while leaving others rather rough.

OH, WHAT A SQUEALING...
SUPERBADD RIDE
STEP ASIDE, OR GET STEPPED ON
ROMPIN', STOMPIN', TROMPIN'

▽ Sketches can take a lot of different forms. Here I've roughed out this wagon in pencil, then come back in with marker for reflections and value, finally finishing it off with a bit of chalk roughly smeared into the top surfaces and windows.

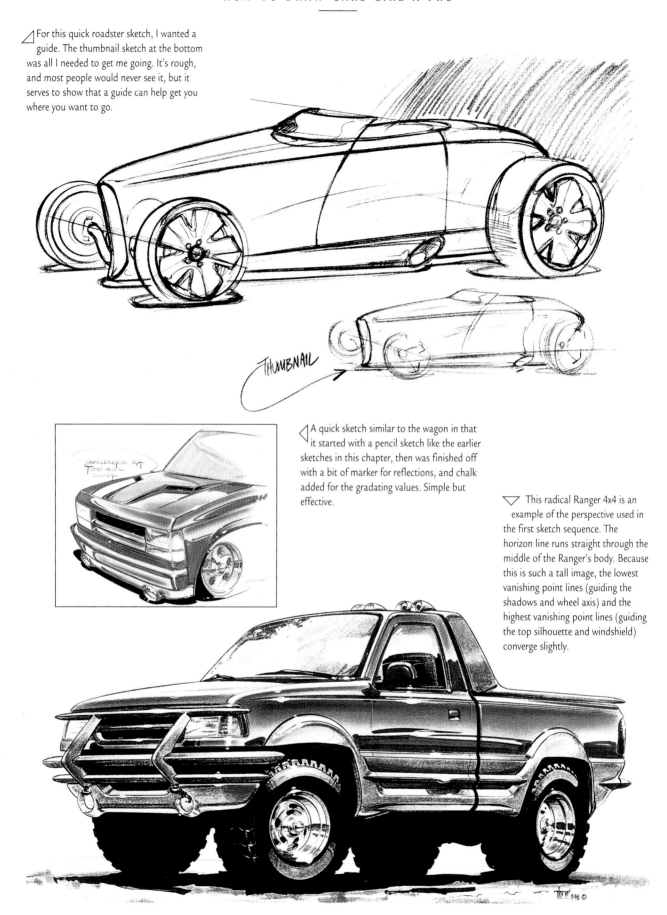

◁ For this quick roadster sketch, I wanted a guide. The thumbnail sketch at the bottom was all I needed to get me going. It's rough, and most people would never see it, but it serves to show that a guide can help get you where you want to go.

THUMBNAIL

◁ A quick sketch similar to the wagon in that it started with a pencil sketch like the earlier sketches in this chapter, then was finished off with a bit of marker for reflections, and chalk added for the gradating values. Simple but effective.

▽ This radical Ranger 4x4 is an example of the perspective used in the first sketch sequence. The horizon line runs straight through the middle of the Ranger's body. Because this is such a tall image, the lowest vanishing point lines (guiding the shadows and wheel axis) and the highest vanishing point lines (guiding the top silhouette and windshield) converge slightly.

△ Another sketch which follows our simple straight-through horizon line, this time of a classic 1957 Chevy. Unlike the Ranger sketch, there is virtually no convergence of vanishing point guidelines. This type of set-up mimics a telephoto camera shot, which tends to flatten the image and pull things forward in perspective. Even so, it looks correct!

Light Source

In Chapter 5, I told you we were done with the technical part of the drawing setup. I lied. Well, sort of. There is another aspect of the setup that could fall into the "technical" side of things: the light source.

When dealing with shading, coloring, shadows, or even where to place certain line emphasis in a line drawing, the light source that is cast on your subject is very important. The light helps to define the shape of the subject, as well as where it is in perspective. And the color of the light source can add a whole new way to dramatically render your subject.

Generally, the lightest portion of the drawing is where the greatest amount of light is cast on the subject. The light values then get progressively darker as the surfaces move away from the core source of the light. Areas in shade are reserved for the darkest values. The easiest way to help you with this is to remember the one-, two-, three-box theory. The top of the box is your lightest or No. 1 value. The side of the box closest to the light source is the No. 2 side, while the side receiving the least amount of light is the No. 3 or darkest side. This is one of those basic rules you must not forget!

Nature has given you a dark base from which to visually support your car by means of the dark shadow cast below it. A warning: Keep your light source in the general area of your head. Sure, it can cast from the right or left side of your subject, but not from behind. Lighting the subject from the rear eliminates the light and the concentrated values reflected as highlights on your car, and only allows you to use a restricted range of values on the car's surfaces. In addition, it casts a big, ugly shadow of the silhouette of your car right in front of it, which can draw the viewer's eye to the shadow instead of the subject. You don't want the shadow to become the big bad hole into which the car is poised to fall.

To take the position of the lighting source one step further, try to have it cast on whatever side of the car it is most advantageous to define. In other words, if you are drawing a front 3/4 view of a car from the driver's side, you may want to have the light source cast more from the right side. This will allow you to cast it along the entire side of the car, yet still give you a bit of light to highlight portions of the front. Or you may prefer lighting from the left to give you the opportunity to cast light along the front, picking up all the

◁ That rising sun in the background of Darrell Mayabb's cool cartoon lets you know where the light source is. Mayabb is a Denver illustrator and cartoonist, and he has to know where the light is coming from to help him make the most of a complicated sketch such as this. It helps him define things like the tire tread, as well as set a foundation for the objects with the use of shadow.

highlights that grilles and air openings allow. You see, the light source is merely another tool you can use to help define the car. You control it for your drawing's greatest benefit.

Recall what I mentioned in Chapter 3 about objects becoming lighter in value and possessing less detail as they move back into the imaginary space created in your drawing. This is somewhat contrary to the fact that as you move farther away from a light source, things get progressively darker. Yet if you observe mountain ranges stepped back, the mountains that are the closest appear darker and come forward from a visual sense. You may want to play with this phenomenon on paper to see what it does.

▽ Besides helping with placement of your
car, shadow can also help you define body
surface and create highlights, such as with this
exaggerated moon-cast setting I created for the
bullet-nose.

◁ For automotive drawing purposes, your light source—be it artificial or the sun—will create a one-, two-, three-box condition. Remember it! It is one of the most basic rules by which to render. It is another part of that imaginary space you are creating on your paper. This is a trick to help you separate the surfaces of your car. The top surface is the lightest, or No. 1 value. The next-closest surface to the light source is the No. 2 surface, which contains a medium value, and finally, the No. 3 surface contains the darkest value. The shadow cast from the object could be considered a fourth value, as it can be an almost black value.

▽ To see the effects of light on a simple object, look at what happens to these cylinders. The first cylinder contains soft surface indication by the use of a core and lack of reflections. A small amount of back lighting helps to separate the back of the cylinder from the shadow. The second cylinder is the same, but with a reflective finish creates harsher highlights and a few reflections. But it follows the same general rules as the first cylinder. With the third cylinder, I've added some random reflections indicating things reflected onto the cylinder that are around it.

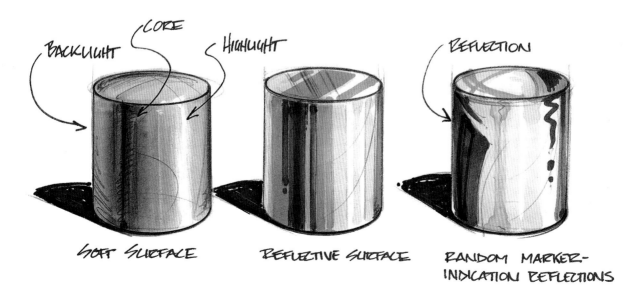

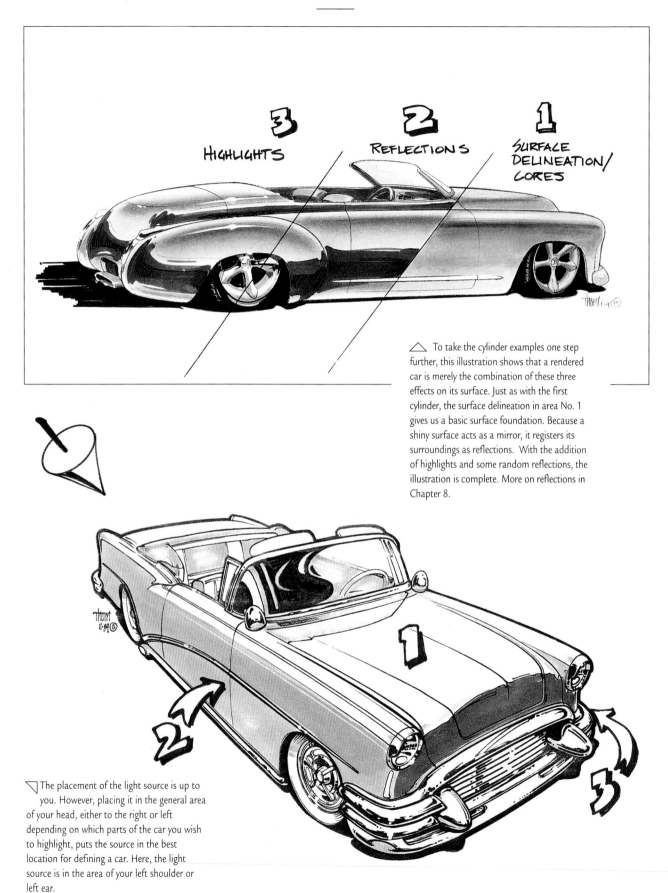

△ To take the cylinder examples one step further, this illustration shows that a rendered car is merely the combination of these three effects on its surface. Just as with the first cylinder, the surface delineation in area No. 1 gives us a basic surface foundation. Because a shiny surface acts as a mirror, it registers its surroundings as reflections. With the addition of highlights and some random reflections, the illustration is complete. More on reflections in Chapter 8.

▽ The placement of the light source is up to you. However, placing it in the general area of your head, either to the right or left depending on which parts of the car you wish to highlight, puts the source in the best location for defining a car. Here, the light source is in the area of your left shoulder or left ear.

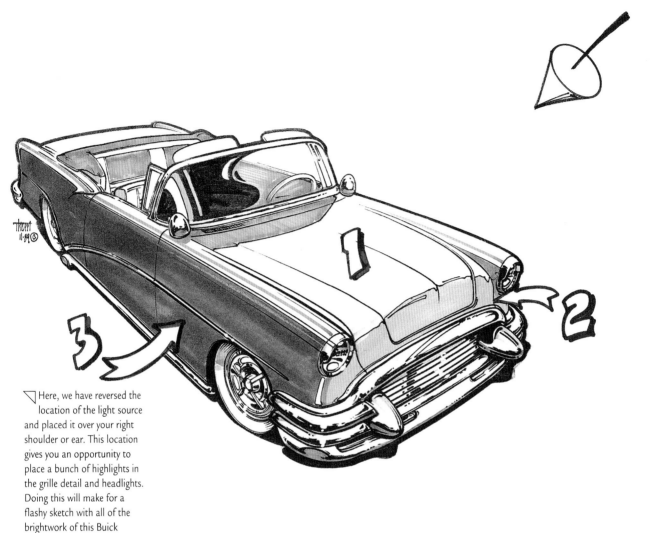

Here, we have reversed the location of the light source and placed it over your right shoulder or ear. This location gives you an opportunity to place a bunch of highlights in the grille detail and headlights. Doing this will make for a flashy sketch with all of the brightwork of this Buick emphasized.

BACKLIGHT

As a general rule, backlighting your car gives you little opportunity to separate and define the surfaces. It also gives you a nasty shadow laying in front while drawing attention away from your car—not good! Since there is no light source hitting the surfaces you see, you have no opportunity to highlight those areas. However, once you have mastered the rules of light and shadow, you can break them. Check out, again, our lead illustration by Darrell Mayabb!

△ As surfaces move away from you, they tend to get lighter in value. Emphasizing this with either line work or rendering surfaces is know as vignetting. Notice how the surfaces closest to you are the darkest values. I've given them a number value to call out what is happening. Values range from a black value of No. 10, to No. 1, which is white. With the exception of the white highlight in the hood and subtle front tire reflection in the hood side, this car is rendered as a dull or soft surface.

A light source
can also help you create
illusions, such as giving the
effect that the front end is way
off the ground in this Lance Sorchik
cartoon. Lance creates some of the most detailed,
but also most distorted cartoons you'll ever see.
Without that shadow, the Vicky looks as if it is climbing
up a hill or sitting on an incline, which makes for a much less
interesting cartoon.

John Bell's cool
one-box van is defined by pencil
shading on the surfaces, with only a faint
indication of reflection on the lower rockers. As the surfaces
move away from you, they vignette. The difference in value between the
front and side surfaces is slight, with a big highlight running through the surface
change to further define the van's shape.

▷ Obviously, you can use light to create special effects in your drawings. Here, Darrell Mayabb was trying for a "setting sun" look—going for that dark-sided, high-contrast look or feel. It also gave Mayabb a chance to render the headlights' beam for an added effect. The long shadows of the bridge guards further define the setting.

Shadows and Reflections

Rendering reflections on the shiny surface of one of my sketches is probably the most enjoyable part of doing the sketch. Knowing how to do it properly takes a certain amount of practice, along with constantly observing exactly what happens to a car's surfaces in the real world. When dealing with reflections on a shiny surface, you must remember that your reflections should not look like stripes painted on the side, but they should look like, well, like reflections. Before you start to render-in your reflections, a good way of looking at the task at hand is to keep in mind that the car's surfaces are really just one huge mirror that is reflecting back what is around it. Carefully observe the surface, visualize what is reflected into it, and you have the basis for your reflection patterns.

Although I show some step-by-step examples in this chapter, there are a few ways you can become equipped to sketch reflections into any surface you choose. The first and best way is to observe. It may be an obvious thing to suggest, but a car's surface changes continually. It's always good to observe the reflections dancing over a surface to see how they react to changes in direction, indentations, and sculpturing. Keep a sketch pad with you and draw what you see as reference for future use. A good selection of reference material freezes in time the way a particular surface change reacts to what is around it.

Combine your observations and reference material, try a simple thumbnail sketch on scratch paper until you are satisfied with what you see, and then apply it to your sketch. The use of a thumbnail sketch is great for several other situations: helping with proportions, placement on the page, backgrounds, and color selections, to name a few. Don't be embarrassed by the need for a thumbnail sketch. I've seen some of the best in the business do it for almost every rendering or painting they do.

Another aid is to have a scale model or toy at your desk that can be used to "stage" certain reflection problems before you begin your sketch. Though the model won't provide exact solutions to your particular car's design (unless it is a model of the car you are sketching), it will help in showing how objects close to the car will reflect on its surfaces, or how its windshield will reflect into the hood. Be careful though, because a model sitting on your drafting table will not mimic a car's real environment.

You will want to show your subject in the best way, by placing it in the "perfect" environment. This may mean you will actually be creating a setting that is almost unreal. If your car has a unique feature that you want to show to its best effect, you may render the car in a special way to highlight this. It may mean running a reflection through that portion of the car to help it pop out, or lighting the car in such a way so that it draws the eye to this area, or possibly by bringing it out with color by adding a warmer tone through it.

Usually, you will not want to copy the reflection detail-for-detail, but rather you will "stylize" your reflections to keep them simple. You don't want your reflections to overpower that sketch; they should blend in and enhance the subject. Fussy, involved reflections may show your ability to copy what happens in the real world, but they don't make for a flashy, punchy drawing. Keep your reflections clean, and your sketch will be, too.

Many of the suggestions that apply to reflections apply to shadows as well. You don't want them to overpower the sketch, or look like they were pasted onto the surface of the car. Like reflections, shadows will need to follow contours and surface changes. As for ground shadows, they will need to be plotted properly so that they help define the bottom of the car, including its tires. This will give it a foundation off which the car can play.

I like to do the ground shadow in solid black. But in doing so, there is always the risk of giving the impression that the car is floating over a big black hole, ready to fall in at any second. This becomes an extension of what we learned in Chapter 7 concerning light sources. Defining the tire's shadow and where the shadow cuts in to separate the wheelwells from the rockers or running boards gives detail and break-up to the shadow's edge. And in doing so, it helps avoid the dreaded black hole syndrome.

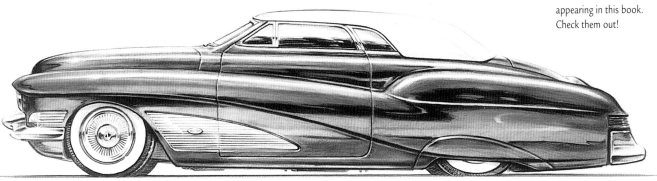

▷ Think of a car as a giant, slightly convoluted mirror. It is reflecting everything that is around it. This becomes another element of the space you are creating when you begin to draw a car. Where is it? What is sitting around it? Where is the light source? You set the stage for your car drawing, and you create that stage to best define your car.

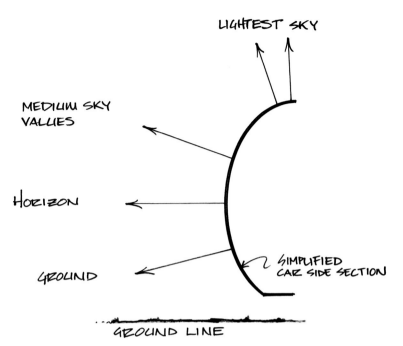

LIGHTEST SKY

MEDIUM SKY VALUES

HORIZON

GROUND

SIMPLIFIED CAR SIDE SECTION

GROUND LINE

▽ Defining the point further, this radical 1963 'Vette has surface changes that pick up conditions within its environment in all different directions. Not only is it picking up reflections, it is picking up cast colors like cool shades from the sky, warm colors from the ground, and highlights from compression of the light source at surface changes.

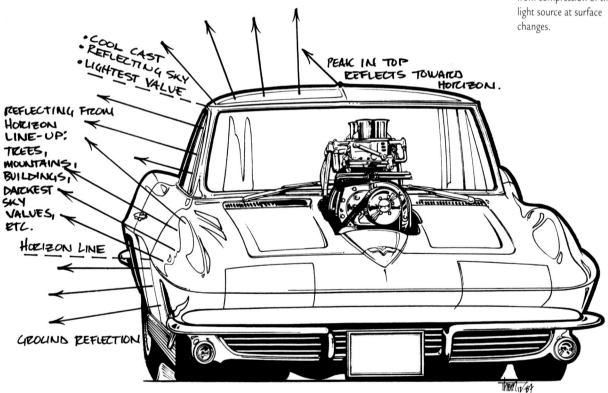

• COOL CAST
• REFLECTING SKY
• LIGHTEST VALUE

PEAK IN TOP REFLECTS TOWARD HORIZON.

REFLECTING FROM HORIZON LINE-UP: TREES, MOUNTAINS, BUILDINGS, DARKEST SKY VALUES, ETC.

HORIZON LINE

GROUND REFLECTION

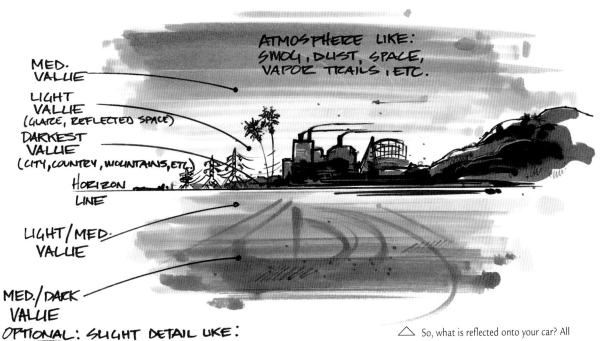

MED. VALUE

LIGHT VALUE (GLARE, REFLECTED SPACE)

DARKEST VALUE (CITY, COUNTRY, MOUNTAINS, ETC.)

HORIZON LINE

LIGHT/MED. VALUE

MED./DARK VALUE

OPTIONAL: SLIGHT DETAIL LIKE: FLOWERS, SIDEWALK CRACKS, COBBLESTONE, ETC.

ATMOSPHERE LIKE: SMOG, DUST, SPACE, VAPOR TRAILS, ETC.

▽ What is happening on the side of you car's body is also happening on its wheels, bumpers, windows . . . everything! This illustration shows you the environment that is being reflected back into the wheel. And since chrome is colorless, the reflection is much more like a mirror.

△ So, what is reflected onto your car? All of what is shown here and more. Anything you wish to reflect is fair game—just make sure you don't confuse the viewer, or your car drawing will end up looking like the dinner in Fluffy's cat bowl. Most of the examples in this book tend to simplify this scene. A car's body will usually compress and stretch out reflections, so that the horizon becomes merely a thin, dark area reflected onto the side of the car.

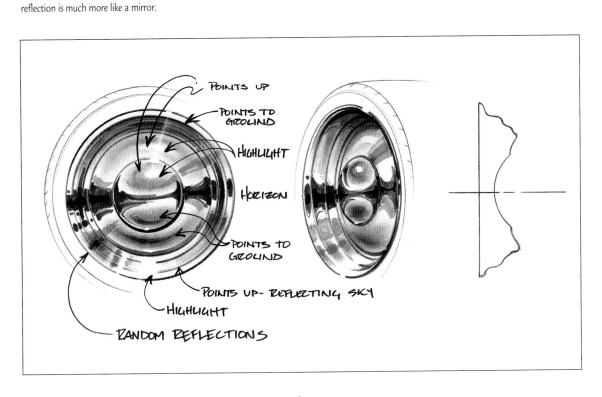

POINTS UP

POINTS TO GROUND

HIGHLIGHT

HORIZON

POINTS TO GROUND

POINTS UP- REFLECTING SKY

HIGHLIGHT

RANDOM REFLECTIONS

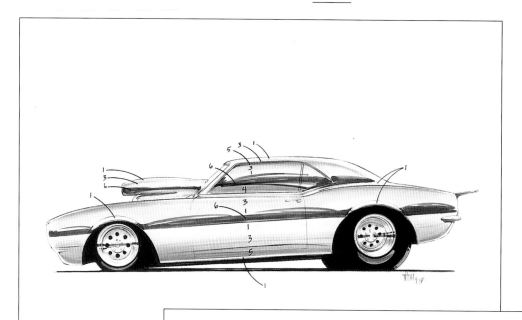

Illustrating this further, we have three different vehicle side views, all reflecting the same environment. The numbers across the bodies indicate values, with No. 1 being white and No. 10 being black. Note that due to the harsh crease in the Camaro's side, the horizon line becomes perfectly flat at the bottom and does not carry down into the area below the crease. Below that crease the surface picks up ground indication only. There are all kinds of variations on these examples, but they are a foundation for every car drawing that includes reflections.

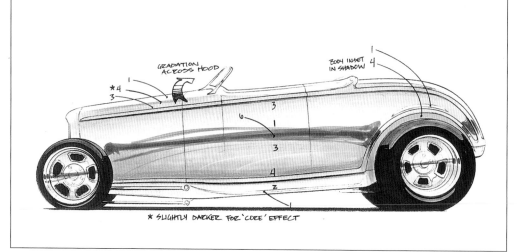

* SLIGHTLY DARKER FOR 'CORE' EFFECT

▽ Not to confuse, but to show how variable reflections can be, I did this sketch to show the subtle surface transition from the deck to the top. To emphasize this feature, I indicated what would amount to a tall wall or building relatively close to the coupe, so the reflection would react in the area of the top transitioning to the deck. The sides of the car lack a certain amount of surface detail as a result, but I get to show off a cool feature of this 1937 Studebaker.

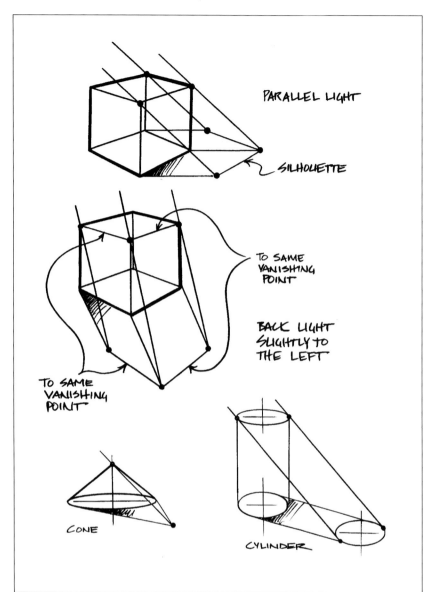

PARALLEL LIGHT

SILHOUETTE

TO SAME VANISHING POINT

BACK LIGHT SLIGHTLY TO THE LEFT

TO SAME VANISHING POINT

CONE

CYLINDER

For shadows, there are some fairly standard rules that you follow to give a proper shadow indication. These simple objects give a general direction that shadows take. Since cars exist outside, the light source will always be the sun. Because it is so far away, the sun's rays are essentially parallel rather than radiating, which makes for easier plotting. A shadow is created when the outermost surfaces or edges to catch the sun's light are cast against another surface, usually the ground.

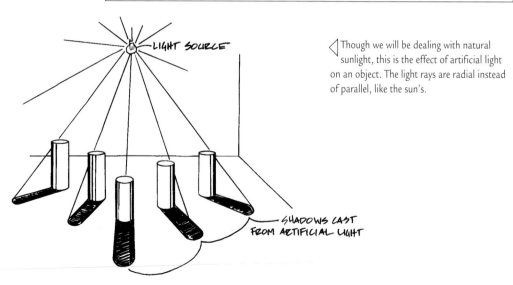

LIGHT SOURCE

SHADOWS CAST FROM ARTIFICIAL LIGHT

Though we will be dealing with natural sunlight, this is the effect of artificial light on an object. The light rays are radial instead of parallel, like the sun's.

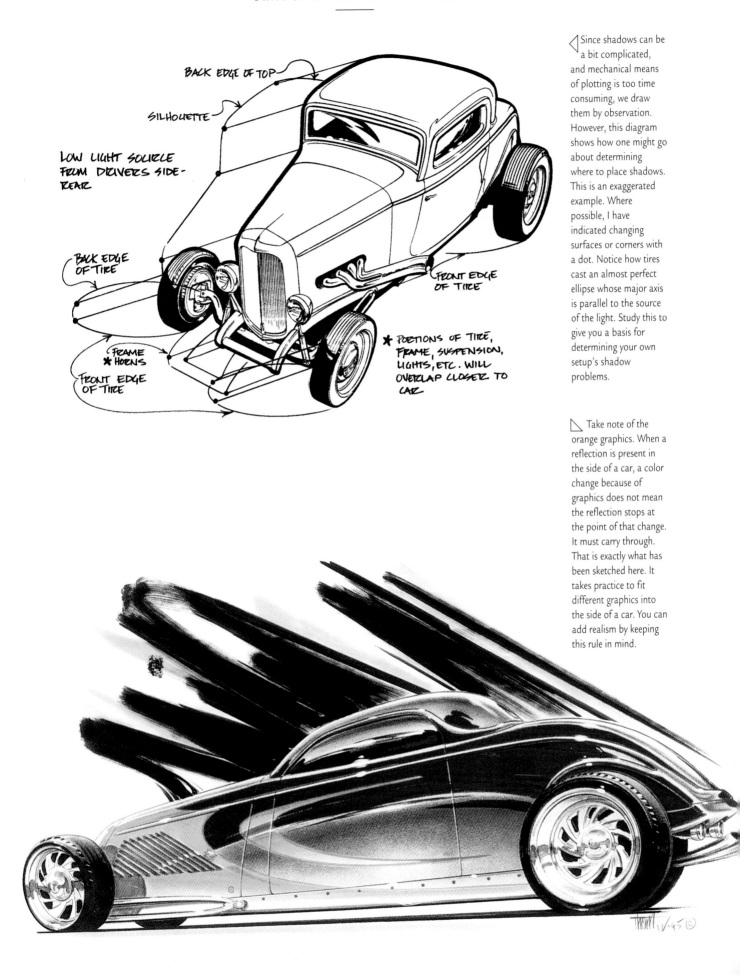

BACK EDGE OF TOP

SILHOUETTE

LOW LIGHT SOURCE
FROM DRIVERS SIDE-
REAR

BACK EDGE
OF TIRE

FRAME
HORNS

FRONT EDGE
OF TIRE

FRONT EDGE
OF TIRE

* PORTIONS OF TIRE,
FRAME, SUSPENSION,
LIGHTS, ETC. WILL
OVERLAP CLOSER TO
CAR

Since shadows can be a bit complicated, and mechanical means of plotting is too time consuming, we draw them by observation. However, this diagram shows how one might go about determining where to place shadows. This is an exaggerated example. Where possible, I have indicated changing surfaces or corners with a dot. Notice how tires cast an almost perfect ellipse whose major axis is parallel to the source of the light. Study this to give you a basis for determining your own setup's shadow problems.

Take note of the orange graphics. When a reflection is present in the side of a car, a color change because of graphics does not mean the reflection stops at the point of that change. It must carry through. That is exactly what has been sketched here. It takes practice to fit different graphics into the side of a car. You can add realism by keeping this rule in mind.

Technique

Every artist has an arsenal of different techniques, but usually one that is his or her bread-and-butter method for drawing. This 1928 Ford roadster pickup incorporates my techniques. Black Verithin pencil, marker, chalk for the gradations, and just a dab of white gouache for the highlights. There are a multitude of variations to this technique, as there are an infinite amount of techniques. With the advent of the computer, this is an understatement!

Technique means the way you actually draw, as well as the medium or utensil used to achieve the drawing. Everyone has a technique lurking inside them. Your technique is your unique combination of seeing things, your dexterity, a heavy or light touch, ability, experience, and even how you feel on a particular day. These, blended with more mechanical circumstances such as what type of pencil or marker you are using, the type of paper you have, and whether you choose to draw in color or black and white, make for the characteristics that define your technique.

Just because you cannot do a drawing exactly like some examples shown in this book does not mean you aren't drawing properly. It just may be your technique starting to show itself. That's great! The difference is what makes your own efforts prized and marketable, instead of just copies of someone else's work.

I've gathered the works of some top automotive designers and artists to illustrate the great diversity in techniques that are possible. Even when similar materials are used for some of the drawings, scrutinize how the differences come through. This is one reason someone wants an Ed Newton sketch instead of a Thom Taylor, or why someone would prefer a cartoon from Dave Bell instead of Lance Sorchik. It's technique: the unique way one draws that attracts a following or creates interest in that particular person's work.

I've also included examples of different techniques applied to an identical subject. This can be a lot of fun to try, and also gives you experience with different media, techniques, and papers. You may find that the same sketch is easier or more rewarding when done one way rather than another. While you may discover that you prefer the work of a particular artist, strive for your own technique. Hopefully, along the way you'll achieve a style that is uniquely yours.

◁ I did these three coupes with completely different techniques. The first version was sketched on Bond paper with only a 747 Verithin pencil. I prefer this over graphite pencils because graphite tends to smear, whereas Verithin pencils don't. In a couple of the highlighted areas I used an eraser to remove pencil and give that hot-spot look.

▷ The second version incorporates the technique I use the most: marker and chalk, with just a bit of Prisma pencil thrown in. The highlights are little dabs of white gouache paint. Gradations are achieved with chalk. More on this in the step-by-step demonstration in Chapter 10. This technique is tighter than that in the previous version.

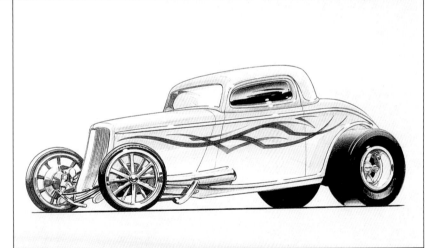

◁ This version is done quickly with a medium marker, then I come back in with colored chalk. Choosing warm colors for the sides and cool colors for the top surfaces really separates the surfaces. The background is a No. 5 gray marker. This technique is the loosest of the three.

△ This cool 1956 Ford was sketched in both a Verithin pencil and black marker. My black marker sketches are meant to resemble India ink techniques, which I hate to work with. Why? Because the stuff is messy and takes a long time to dry, and I like to get through a sketch as quickly as I can. One trick to speed up a pen-and-ink sketch is by using a hair dryer. These black and white line sketches work great for silkscreen-printed T-shirts.

▽ The same car in a 747 Verithin technique—minus the rear wing. The shadow was darkened with a black marker and the area around the taillight was juiced up with a medium gray marker. Both of these sketches were done on Bond paper.

▽ This sketch started out as an India ink drawing, then was scanned into his Mac to achieve the values, smoke, and blurs or tracers coming off of the back.

▽ Cartoonist
   Dave Deal uses
a number of techniques, even scanning some of his sketches into his Macintosh computer to create still more variations on his techniques. The first example is very typical of his pencil sketch technique, but the background and windshield gradations have been generated on his Mac.

△ Frankenstude is a restyled 1951 bullet-nose Studebaker I designed a few years ago. The drawing uses one of my favorite techniques, but one I seldom use. It is a combination of colored Prisma pencils, black marker, and a little gouache paint on dark purple matte board. Pick a matte board or Canson paper the color of the car you wish to draw, then use lights and darks to achieve a finished drawing. For a light-colored car, you'll be working with darker values, and with a darker car you'll be using almost all light values to get this or a similar effect. Sketch the car lightly in a value close enough to that of the board so you don't need to erase your guide lines later on. Most of the car styling studios used a similar technique back in the 1930s and 1940s.

▽ The same car done in black marker and chalk. In this case, you are starting with a white sheet of Bond paper, so you are working in progressively darker values as you go. Starting with a clean white sheet of paper is the typical way you will render, be it in pencil, marker, or mud. That is why it can be fun to shift gears and work with colored paper or board.

△ John Bell's technique for this cool GM-out-of-control sketch is similar to the Frankenstude sketch done on black paper. Bell adds drama and interest to this fun drawing with gouache and yellow Prisma pencil to give the impression that the headlights are on. The "blurred" Bluestreaks really give the impression of movement.

◁ My assignment: to
▽ mimic the
airbrushed glamour of
1940s styling studios in
my illustrations for the
1988 Francis Ford
Coppola film, *Tucker: The
Man and His Dream*. Back
in the 1930s and 1940s,
the Detroit studios used
high-contrast airbrushed
renderings on black
backgrounds to achieve
this rich, pop-off-the-
page look.

Color

Color enriches a sketch with added interest and dimension. When used effectively, it is an eye-grabbing tool. It draws the eye into the sketch and helps give an added dimension, thanks to a few simple tricks you can try. However, color can just as easily ruin a sketch if overworked or used in the wrong manner.

Having a good range of colors available, whether they are markers, pencils, or chalks, helps you blend and highlight color with color. If your funds are limited but you're itching to try color in your drawings, start with a range of colored pencils or markers within a particular color, such as blue. Building up or "layering" your drawings works better with a range of one or two particular colors. Having a good range of one color is better than a beginners' set consisting of a green, a red, a blue, etc. Then, if you feel like you want to develop this further, you can begin to get into other ranges of colors to gradually fill out your pallet.

When it comes to color, there are color theories like the classic Munsell and Ostwald color systems (used in most art schools), things like tinting, contrasting colors, complementary colors, and so on. But for drawing a car, we are not dealing so much with systems or theory as we are trying to depict

a car in a particular color. It's not as simple as it sounds, but is fairly easy to master. So let's concentrate on car color theory and leave the other information for another time and another book, perhaps one on color that you find at your local library or bookstore.

Cool colors such as blue, purple, or green tend to recede or go back into a perspective sketch. Warm colors such as yellow or red or orange come forward in a sketch.

A trick when doing a color sketch: Use a warmer version of the car color for areas closest to the viewer, which is you. Similarly, to get portions of the car to go back into the drawing's imaginary perspective space, use a cooler version of the car's color. And as you learned in Chapter 3, as you go back into that space, you will also want to make the car lighter in value. These changes in color should be very subtle and used more as a veiled trick than something overt. If the change is too obvious, it becomes distracting and you lose the effect you are trying to achieve. It may even give the illusion that the car is painted in a blend of one color to another on its surface. Once you master the use of color on a car, this might be a fun experiment to try. But for now, let's concentrate on a single color.

Here's another trick to use with color: Since a car is almost always viewed outdoors, the sky reflects a subtle blue cast over the surfaces of the car that point upward. But don't forget that those surfaces pointing up also get lighter, as in the one-, two-, three-box examples in Chapter 7. And just as the sky reflects from above, the ground reflects into the lower portions of a car body. These ground reflections will cast a warm or yellow/brown tone into those lower surfaces. With the cooler sky-tones in the upper surfaces and the warm ground-tones in the lower portions of the body, your rendering will start to take on some real-world characteristics. As you start thinking about the use of warm and cool tones, try to experiment to decide how far you want to go to introduce these cast tones to your drawing. Too little and you hardly notice, while too much makes for a strange "circus wagon" look to your rendering.

There is another pit to avoid falling into when applying color to your drawing: If you are too timid with your colors, you can give the illusion that the car is made of tinted glass. The drawing takes on a characteristic of being visually lighter than air. So when you lay in color, try to remember to keep "volume" in the drawing. The car is a very heavy, solid object. You want it to have that appearance in your drawing. If the car is a light color to begin with, the variation in value will become less. The No. 1 side of your imaginary box may be only slightly lighter than your No. 2 side. I know this is a lot to remember, so try these suggestions a little bit at a time. Keep referring back to this and other chapters for these useful tips.

▽ We want to establish our harsher reflections first because they establish the darkest values you will render on the body. This becomes your base for values so you know how far to go with your chalk or airbrush gradations later on. These reflections could have stopped at the front fender to help give us a more disparate two-three-side (remember the one-, two-, three-box?). Because this view ended up much like a telephoto shot with the front pulled out so far, both the side and front are facing our imaginary horizon line, so the horizon reflections would carry through both the front and side. Lay in the red marker with a light touch and keep the strokes random looking, even if you plot them out to a fine degree. Random doesn't mean sloppy. Notice the windshield reflected onto the cowl.

I like to run a secondary reflection into the horizon reflection but you may choose to omit this step. I do this to help break up the main reflection, and to help give it a form of gradation. It also adds a bit more interest. This secondary reflection is usually a value or two darker than the main one. Keep it simple and well within the main reflection. Some artists, including Charlie Smith, darken the upper edge of the horizon reflection. It is probably a bit more literal, and it works equally well. Once you are done with your sketch, you may want to go back in with this darker marker and slightly darken up some areas of your sketch for better definition. Tread lightly. If you go darker by one value and don't feel that it is dark enough, you can always go darker. You can't go lighter.

I'm doing a couple of steps here. One is to fill in the tire/shadow area, grille opening, and dark areas between the wheel spokes with black marker. Shadows aren't usually black, but it is easier for me to do. If you would like, you can use black for the tires and run a No. 6 for the ground shadow. The other step is to start filling in the wheel details with a No. 5 cool gray marker. I'm using the No. 5 for the undersides of the wheel. There is also a bit of No. 4 cool gray carrying through the fender reflections into the headlight covers.

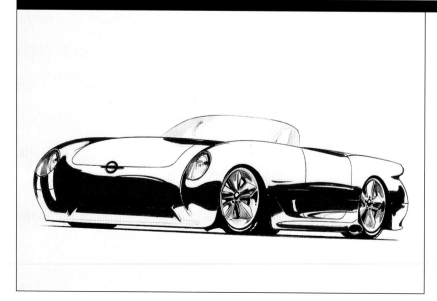

Horizon reflection, ground tones, and sky reflections have been added to the wheels. While our sky blue marker is out, let's run some sky reflection into the far part of the windshield. This would indicate something out in front and to the right side of the car that is reflected into the far portion of the windshield. Since I want to push the point that this is glass and it's hanging out there in the air, I chose sky blue. If "that thing" out there in front of the car was green or yellow, then you could justify those colors reflecting onto the windshield. But that would be a bit confusing, right? So sky blue makes a bit more sense. Headlight horizon lines and other reflections are added, and the same justification for our blue windshield reflection yields us the gray one on the driver's side.

We are now finished with the marker portion of the sketch. It's time to get messy. We want to mask off the car and a bit of the background so that we can put in our gradating tones. If you are a real slob you may want to mask off the entire background. A clean background could give you a whole new reputation. But you and I will know it was just the masking film. For mask material try drafting tape, Frisket film in sheets or rolls, or Nitto tape, which looks like Scotch tape but has less tack. The Nitto tape is shown here. A less expensive way to mask is to use tracing paper larger than the image. Spray mount the back, let it dry thoroughly and slap it down. No matter which mask you use, you will want to cut the mask out of all of the areas of the car that are still in white. A sharp X-ACTO knife and a delicate touch are needed here. Especially on Bond or rag paper, be careful that you don't cut through.

With the mask now removed from the areas in which we'll be working, we will lay in our base color with chalk or airbrush. To help enrich the red we will ultimately use, I chose yellow chalk as a base. If you are doing a black car—which can be the most difficult color to render—you would use turquoise or blue at this stage. The trick with chalk is to cushion the underside of your drawing with a pad of Bond or tracing paper. This helps the chalk flow better, and the stick won't scratch the paper—trust me. I just rub the chalk right into the areas I wish to work. If you are doing this on board, be careful not to scratch the surface with the stick. The gauze pads available for working chalk seem useless to me. Rubbing in the chalk with one of them removes too much material. Once the stick of chalk is rubbed in, I feather it out with my finger. Make sure you wash your hands often at this stage.

With the yellow feathered in, I come back with the red chalk. Again, for a black rendering, you would now come in with black chalk. Here, I've rubbed the red stick into the areas into which I have just feathered the yellow. The excess red you see can either be rubbed into the drawing or blown or brushed off after you are done with this stage.

◁ It takes a deft touch, but you will get the hang of rubbing in the red with your finger(s). Practice first, maybe do a quick thumbnail to see how far you want to go with the color gradation. It's starting to look like a real car now.

▷ I can never control the chalk to any great extent. Because of this, I merely block in the areas I wish to have a gradation in and come back with a pencil-type of pink eraser to eliminate chalk from surfaces that face up, or to give me a preliminary highlight. Cut the end off with an X-ACTO knife for a really clean, sharp tool. Once it gets rounded off a bit, you just cut more off. The fender lips were done this way. I like to run those eraser highlights right through the core of the chalk gradations for added sparkle and interest. I have observed this in reality, but also experienced it missing in certain circumstances. These types of details come from observation and what you feel works best for the drawing. In some ways, this kills the clean, smooth gradation you have worked so hard to execute. If you feel this way, you can omit this step.

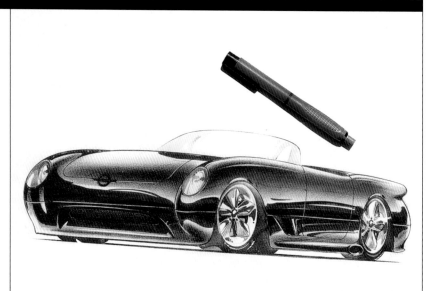

◁ Run a little spray fixative over the sketch to help hold in the chalk, because we will be laying another mask over some of these areas. Once the fixative is dry, run a mask over the windshield area. Cut out the mask where the windshield is. With light blue chalk, I lay a gradation over the entire windshield. The light area is picking up the hottest point in the sky, which is our light source. As the windshield points out toward the sky, away from our light, it starts to pick up the color of the sky. If we were creating a late afternoon setting, this might be orange or even purple. Try it and see what works best for the imaginary environment you have created for this sketch. You may want to play with some gradating blue in the wheels at this stage. If you don't like what you come up with, it's easy to erase!

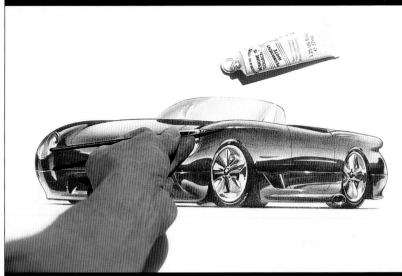

The final touch is to throw in some "pigeon highlights" with white gouache and a No. 0 or No. 1 sable brush. The better the brush, the more pointed the end. Use a jar of water at the art store to test it out. If the end is blunt, move on to the next brush. The best is Windsor-Newton Series 7 sable brushes. The price is out of this world, but you only cry once when you buy the best. Mix a little water with the gouache for a nice consistency, and lay in the highlights like an elongated football. Try to keep them from looking like a blob of real pigeon droppings!

For the background, you'll need to mask off the car again. Once this is done, scrape some chalk into the background with your X-ACTO knife. Next, soak some Bestine solvent thinner into a pad, or in this case, a toilet tissue, and streak it through the area where you have sprinkled the chalk. Leave some white areas if you can, and try to mix two or three colors of chalk into the background for an interesting mix. Oil sticks can be used if you don't like the smell of Bestine. Other examples of this smear background technique can be found in the book, so pay attention to what they do and where they go.

The finished product looks great, if I do say so. You can go crazy with detail from this point. Finite tire tread, refining wheel reflections and detail, brake detail, interior detail (if you see it—we don't here), and on and on. This can take you anywhere from 2 to 10 hours, depending on how fast you are, how many thumbnails you create, and how many times you're interrupted by your butler, maid, mother, or spouse.

Presentation

You've got a pretty decent sketch of a Viper GTS coupe but you need some way to enhance it rather than just letting it stand alone. This can be as simple as adding a background or border, or as elaborate as positioning it with buildings, people, and cars in a realistic setting. While there are many ways to come up with an enhancement for your sketch, we are merely touching the surface with these examples.

One thing to keep in mind with backgrounds is that they can become part of the illustration itself if they are placed too close to the subject. This can be good or bad—depending on what you are trying to accomplish. If the background is too close, you have the option of casting a small amount of its color into those surfaces of the car that are either near the background, or pointed in its general direction.

The other option is to reflect part of the background into the car. If you choose to do this, you must do it in a way that keeps the car and its background separated. Again, that background is only an enhancement. It should not over-power your work. Elaborate framing devices or backgrounds are best left with the Baroque works of the 1600s. We're way past that, man!

▷ Usually, I'll do a background to tie together objects in a drawing, or as a means to help the main image bounce off of the page. In the case of the *Jade Grenade* shown here, it was the latter. And I can be a bit lazy, so I tend to view the background as a bit of cheating to help the drawing, instead of a drawing itself. The blue in the background ties in with the cool greens I used in the Harley, and both the blue and black are dark enough to punch out the bike.

△ In this case, the art director wanted a quick background that would help give the impression that this scene was taking place in the future. And he liked the *Pontiac Salsa* show car so much that he wouldn't let me vary my sketch much from the real car. Oh, well! Though the car is almost all chalk, the background is pure marker and so are the people.

▽ Steve Stanford and I share Sketchpad duties at *Rod & Custom* Magazine from time to time. Besides the great design and rendering abilities Stanford possesses, he incorporates some cool, simple marker backgrounds to help set a mood and enhance the main image. They really don't take much time, and sometimes they give Stanford an excuse to reflect the background image or color into the car for added effect. This Impala SS Chevy truck shows us just such a case.

▽ Another instance of Stanford's fun backgrounds comes with this new Bug for *Hot VWs* Magazine. When you do a background that ends so abruptly, watch out for tangencies to the car. You want to be able to separate the car from the background, not make them appear as one image. This is another reason why this particular background works.

Presentation is what Greg Tedder's work is all about. These color comps are done entirely in marker. He uses the marker as a wash, blending the colors together to create his gradations. Tedder approaches reflections in a very unique way, which is why these are so great to look at and why a Greg Tedder sketch looks like a Greg Tedder sketch. Though these are meant as guides for silkscreened apparel, we're looking at them here for their presentation quality. The computer-generated type, combined with the main and background images, creates an entire presentation. Imagine how this Caprice might look without the elements around it.

Though this car is black, the light blue outline helps to separate it from the black background. Again, note how the colors are bounced around to help move the eye as it keys into a particular color. The elements help to frame the images, without putting a boring border around the drawing.

△ Color is thrown all over in this Tedder comp. He works the red of the Gee Bee plane into the wheels and foreground of this 1938 Ford. The turquoise in the Ford is bounced back into the lines behind the plane. Bouncing these colors around keeps them from becoming isolated and gives a continuity to the sketch.

▽ When trying a multiple car set-up, placement becomes critical. Here, Darrell Mayabb leads your eyes from one image to another by the arrangement of the cars and the directions in which they are pointing. It is interesting to see how some of the images overlap. Some are framed with a border, and some incorporate a secondary element (such as a person) to add interest and break things up.

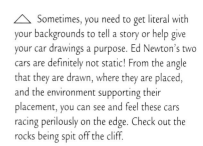

△ Sometimes, you need to get literal with your backgrounds to tell a story or help give your car drawings a purpose. Ed Newton's two cars are definitely not static! From the angle that they are drawn, where they are placed, and the environment supporting their placement, you can see and feel these cars racing perilously on the edge. Check out the rocks being spit off the cliff.

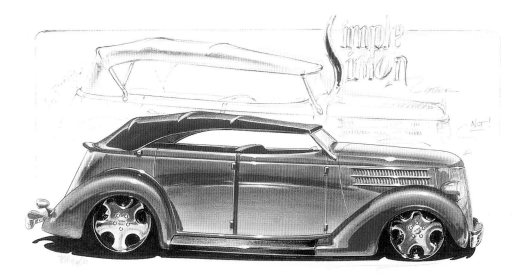

▽ The presentation of this Charlie Smith rendering is great because he worked the two cars in the background that inspired his original design. Sometimes when you are dealing with obscure cars like this, it's helpful to the viewer to enlighten them as to what the whole piece is based on. In this case it's a 1953 Studebaker.

△ A background can work to show how dramatic a design modification can be, as with this 1936 Ford phaeton sketch. Since the top and windshield were the main changes to the design, shifting it up the underlay and sketching the stock top configuration was simple. It graphically shows the difference and adds interest by using it as a background.

△ Sometimes all it takes to add drama and interest to your drawing is to place it at a skewed angle . Charlie Smith enhanced his car rendering by tipping the horizon line. To take it a step farther, Smith added a smeared background to give the look of movement. All these tricks take the car away from a static, staid look.

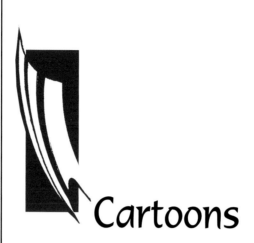

Cartoons

Virtually every time you freehand sketch a car, you have created a cartoon. Why? Because you have exaggerated the car or drawn it slightly out of proportion even if you didn't intend to. Stretching, squishing, leaning, and tilting—the more there is, the more you've removed your sketch from reality. But it sure is fun. Some find it easier to draw a cartoon of a car, while others find it a bit more difficult than doing a straightforward sketch.

If you find yourself drawn to this naturally, that's fine. For those who wish to enter the zany world of cartoon fun, but find it a bit hard to grasp, you may want to concentrate on first drawing a car as well as you can. Once you reach a certain comfort level, you can then ease over into the cartoon world. By taking your ability to draw well-proportioned sketches and then exaggerating them a bit, you can explore changes in the relationships of elements that make up a car sketch. Chopping a top is the easiest proportion change to sketch. Exaggerating the sizes of the wheels or tires is another. Body proportions heightened or reduced, elongated or squeezed, can give your drawing any feeling you may want to convey.

Rather than have me blabber on, check out the accompanying examples, culled from some of the best in the business. Many of these artists have been doing this for more than 30 years, so don't be intimidated by the high quality displayed here.

Study what makes these drawings so special, and practice giving your cartoons that same look. Notice how each of the artists shown here has his own unique style. Strive to come up with a look that is uniquely yours. But most important—have fun!

Dave "Big" Deal

Deal is one of the premier cartoonists in the country. The fact that he can read, write, and speak in languages as diverse as Hebrew and Mayan only adds to his intrigue. Deal uses a number of techniques to get that Big Deal look, relying mainly on pencil for one type and India ink for the other. To fill in values, he may stick with pencil if he started with it or go to a marker wash. Lately, he's been scanning the outline into his Mac and rendering it in from there.

Dave
"Big" Deal

Dave "Henry Hirise" Bell

Dave "Henry Hirise" Bell

Bell has been doing Henry Hirise cartoons in the back of *Street Rodder* Magazine for just about every issue published. In addition, Bell does posters, T-shirts, and even pinstriping out of his St. Paul, Minnesota, studio. His style is lighthearted and fun, and done exclusively in India ink on heavy paper stock. Sometimes, to make a slight correction or two, he'll use some white gouache to paint out the offending mark.

Ed Newton

Ed Newton

Newton was the artist behind all of those great Ed "Big Daddy" Roth monster designs from the 1960s. I tried unsuccessfully during my youth to copy his technique, but never had any luck. Know why? It's because he uses a brush to do all of that great thick and thin linework. His more recent work involves a lot of airbrush, marker, India ink (both drawn and sprayed through an airbrush), and even gouache as in the case of the monster on black Canson paper.

Darrell Mayabb

Darrell Mayabb

Cartooning seems almost a sideline for Mayabb. He's an artist in the truest sense; his problem is that his love of cars gets in the way of him taking the fine art as far as it could really go. But that makes it all the better for those of us who love to see his work. His cartoons work in a lot of mixed media including pencil, India ink, watercolor washes, marker, airbrush, gouache, and more. Lately he has been working in some computer rendering. His cartoons show up regularly in many automotive magazines, including *Hot Rod*.

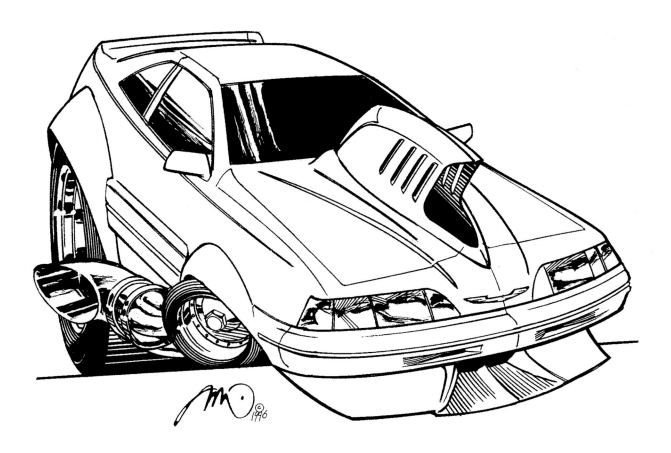

Lance "Jersey Suede" Sorchik

Lance "Jersey Suede" Sorchik

Sorchik is a true hot rod artist. How else could you explain the kind of detail he includes in every cartoon? He uses India ink almost exclusively, but we are also including a color illustration he did with an airbrush. For gradations, Lance uses a method called stippling. This involves putting down lots of little dots in differing sizes and proximity to achieve a gray tone. He also has the ability to twist an old car more than I've ever seen. He knows what parts to emphasize or exaggerate, and which proportions to distort for a really lively cartoon. Sorchik is a high school art teacher in Sussex County, New Jersey, whose cartoons can be seen regularly in *Rodder's Digest* magazine.

Lance
"Jersey Suede"
Sorchik

Mark Balfe

Mark Balfe

St. Paul's Mark Balfe has been doing cartooning for a number of years. I first became aware of him at a Rat Fink Reunion in San Francisco, where he was introduced to me by none other than Ed "Big Daddy" Roth. At the time, Balfe was doing a lot of Roth's T-shirt art, which was a take-off on the style that Ed Newton developed back in the 1960s. You will notice that besides the Roth T-shirt style, Balfe also has a humorous style adapted as his own. He is a brush illustrator, meaning these were all drawn with a brush, not a pen.

Thom Taylor

Thom Taylor

I've included a few of my own cartoons for comparison. Though I don't do a lot of this type of work, I love doing it when the opportunity arises. I have the pleasure of drawing the Frog Follies rod run art every year, with hot rods and cold frogs depicted in some sort of setting. All my cartoon art is done with a marker or fine line pen on Bond paper or Crescent board. I guess I'm a slob in a hurry, for India ink is too slow and messy for me. But you can't beat the blackness and crispness that it gives you, which is why a lot of the artists featured here use the stuff.

Thom Taylor

Cutaways

△ For inspiration, we have included West's first cutaway, done in 1968 right out of high school. The Herrera & Sons AA/GS 51 Austin was published in *Popular Hot Rodding* later that year. Compare this with some of West's more recent drawings.

A cutaway of a car is like one of those detailed "inside the human body" drawings with the skeleton, organs, and a virtual road map of veins and muscles: all the guts and glory.

If you've ever marveled at the complexity of a cutaway drawing, you've probably wondered how the artist did it. Although I have only done a few, I feel that if you know your perspective, have an interest in things of a mechanical nature, and own a good camera, then you are able to do a cutaway. Oh, yeah—you need to set aside a lot of time. Despite what you might think, drawings of this nature take quite a while to set up and even longer to complete.

The best subject to choose is one in which you have a lot of interest (for you'll be living with it for quite a while), and one on which you can get the greatest amount of reference material. That means being able to take a ton of pictures of as much of the car as possible. A popular car with lots of magazine coverage might be a good subject simply for this reason. You may want to consider a race car as a first try; with the body removed, many of the internals are revealed for which you need photographic reference for an accurate, detailed drawing. If your choice has limited reference available, then you will need to track down the information. Illustrator Tom West uses more than 200 photos for a single cutaway! When it comes to reference material, you can never have enough.

It is this build-up of material that gives you a good foundation for any cutaway endeavor. The first step is to draw the body and the frame separately on tissue or tracing paper, in the same perspective. This begins the preliminary drawing version. Almost universally this perspective will be a front elevation, which tips the car up enough to show most of what is going on from front to back. You may want to trace this initial attempt from a photo. From here, it is a step-by-step process of building up the components. Draw them on separate pieces of tissue paper, so that if you make a mistake, you don't

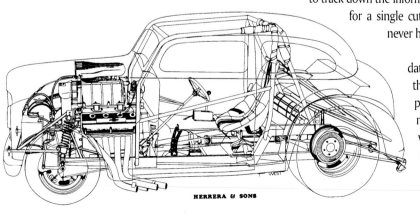

HERRERA & SONS

Tom West

Tom West has been kind enough to include a myriad of his great cutaways along with a brief rundown of exactly how he goes about completing one of these drawings. The key is to have lots of film, time, patience to construct the drawing, and the reference photos for an endeavor such as this.

West begins by shooting an overall exterior shot that he uses to frame the individual detail shots he gets. A tripod is moved from position to position with doors and hood open, wheels on and off, removable panels on and off, etc. Using a photo enlarger, he creates a base photo which is a composite of the individual shots. The enlarger is locked in position so that the negatives are changed in the holder. The resulting patchwork quilt of overlaying photos gives West his base from which to work. If this is cost prohibitive, you can try enlarged photocopies. They can be pasted together and then copied again to eliminate the cut lines. He tries to keep the original's size at around 36 inches for drawing and sight convenience.

He shoots a lot of reference photos for those areas covered by body panels or other components. There can literally be hundreds. These shots are used to help determine details and proportions. Get a lot of shots of the less-obvious areas of the car that may be hidden at first glance. You'd be amazed how much they can help once you get into the drawing.

The cutaways are done on polyester drawing film placed over his photo print, with the aid of a light table. The actual line work is done with different pencil lead weights from 4H to HB. Because the lead smears easily, he tries to cover as much of the film as possible, exposing only those areas he is working on, or needs for reference. Corrections are made with a vinyl eraser.

The actual image is done from the outside in, starting with the body and in toward whatever comes next, such as a tire/wheel combo, or header pipe, or radiator. One component should naturally progress to the neighboring components. If you get stuck, you can always move to another area and develop it while you figure out how to continue in the problem area. Keep your images fairly basic, so that once you have blocked out the entire cutaway, you can come in and detail it to the level you feel comfortable doing. West uses the guides and templates mentioned earlier in this book.

have to junk everything you've created up to this point. Obviously, they must all be drawn in a scale and perspective that tie into what you have drawn for the body and frame.

Since you will probably be playing one component off another and scaling from one to another, you should start sketching in the big components such as the engine and transmission; consider adding the wheels and tires soon, since many components are connected to these items. Sometimes you can cheat a little by using a copy machine to reduce or enlarge a sketch that is too large or small. In special cases, you can probably tilt a component sketch that is slightly out of perspective and it will look right, although you know it is slightly off.

What you end up with is one huge, layered puzzle that will serve as a basis for the final version. With the use of a light table you will do your final drawing with all of these earlier, separate drawings placed together. From here on it is just a matter of drawing each component in place, in perspective, and with a pen or pencil. Shadows and/or color can be added once this stage of the drawing is completed. In my color cutaway, I found it necessary to outline certain components in a dark gray to help separate them from neighboring components. You may or may not choose to try this; it works for me.

Technically, this is one of the most difficult drawings to execute but it is also one of the most rewarding. It can be both informative and entertaining and you will find that some people can stare transfixed at your work of art. You may find that you will want to deviate from the steps I have laid out, which is just fine. What works for me may not work for you since this is such an involved creation, so don't feel tied to these steps. Good luck!

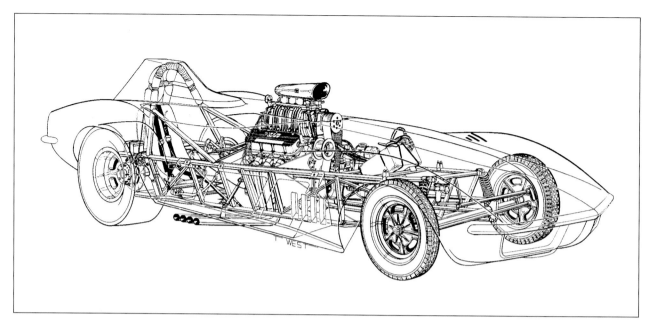

△ By West's 12th cutaway, the incorporation of thick and thin line weights and less shading makes for a nice drawing. This was also his first for *Car Craft* Magazine. Now he wishes he could have filled in behind the front wheels and the engine plate. Without the photo reference, there was little he could do. The lesson: get lots of reference photos!

▽ The 30th cutaway drawing produced by West incorporates a bit of the flag paint graphics into the body, to help spice up those areas where there really is nothing. The Cook & Foster *Damn Yankee* Barracuda Funny Car was published in the October 1971 *Drag Racing USA*.

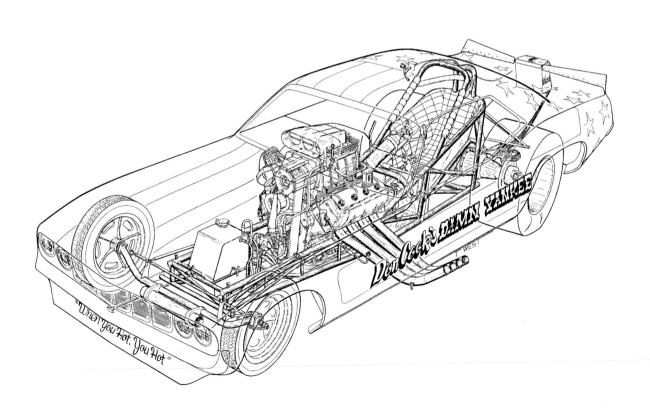

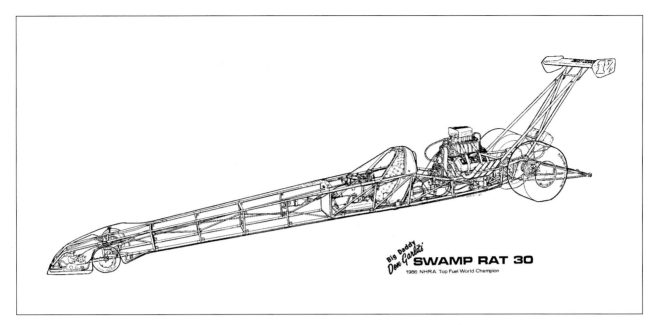

△ This cutaway was hanging in the Smithsonian Institution as a backdrop for the display of the actual Garlits *Swamp Rat XXX* Top Fuel Dragster. It's the 35th cutaway drawn by West, completed in 1987.

▽ A car I have a personal interest in because I designed it for Joe Hrudka, the Coddington-built *Chezoom* was a difficult car for West to draw. There was little time to shoot reference photography on the car; this overall view was a result of the weird camera angle and lens required due to the cramped space where the car was built. I can relate because I had to call certain styling shots for the car with extremely limited viewing space. As the unique angle of the cutaway has grown on West, so too have some of the compromised styling modifications grown on me.

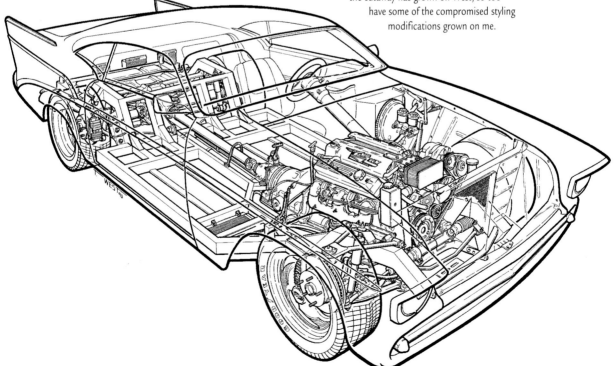

◺ Another one of my hot rod designs: The *Speedwagon* is based on a 1932 Ford built by Dan Fink. This cutaway was commissioned by Fink for publication in *Street Rodder* Magazine in September of 1993. As West told me, the view is high enough to see a lot of the chassis detail, but low enough to see the unique proportions of the *Speedwagon*.

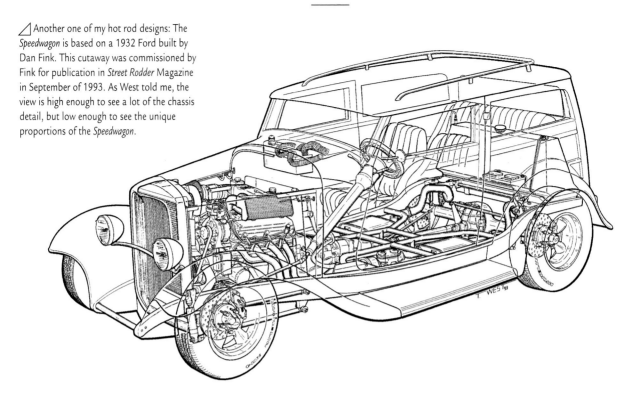

▽ Drawn for Haynes Publishing, this 1994 Ford E350 Econoline van is one of West's favorites. Most of the reference material was hit-and-miss because the van was assembled, so it was impossible to get good photos of certain hidden portions. Though an uninspiring vehicle, it makes for a great cutaway.

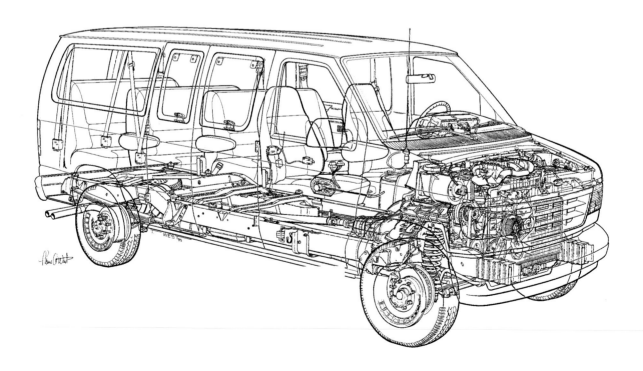

△ Yes, I've done a few of these myself.
Commissioned by Gary Newton for his SOHC
"T" Roadster, it was drawn on matte board
predominately with Prisma color pencils. The
angle is descriptive, allowing for a good view of
what is going on inside the car. I found that a
medium gray outline of the components
helped them pop out a bit. Though I don't
normally recommend outlining things, it works
here. Completed in 1989, it is probably the
last cutaway I'll ever do! But don't let me
discourage you—this could be the start of a
great career for you in cutaway drawing.

Interiors

Sketching an interior can be a little like doing a cutaway in that you are sketching several separate things within the confines of a particular perspective. Instrument parts and components, seats, and door hardware are part of a larger whole. With interiors, however, there is much less to create, and much of what you create has a similar surface finish. And that finish is almost never shiny, so watch it. Since I don't regularly do seats or dashes, I have to be careful that I don't give the impression they are made from a shiny material. Rendering a hard, cold surface does not make for an inviting car interior.

Because there aren't any highlights to help you define or separate surfaces, you are forced to be a little more precise with your one-, two-, and three-box lighting. Defining each undulation and surface change will help you visually describe your interior. And the light source will determine shadows, which become another tool to help you define surfaces. Shadows also add a darker, or No. 4 value, to complement your No. 1, No. 2, No. 3 values.

The easy part of an interior sketch is that, for the most part, you will lay it out in one-point perspective. Tipping it up allows a better view and is the preferred choice for the sketch setup. What you decide to leave out can be as interesting as what you leave in. Since one seat mimics the other, it may not be necessary to show both, at least not in a great amount of detail. Also, using a heavy border or other stopping device can keep you from having to render an entire car interior, including pillows and windows—it may give you a graphic element or background off which you can play the interior.

A trick to add interest to your interior sketch is to indicate a texture of a subtle (or wild) cloth pattern. It allows you to add a "layer" to help define the surfaces still further. In addition, it helps to define the perspective when you lessen the detail of your pattern or texture as it moves back into the perspective distance of your sketch.

▽ This sketch is good in terms of layout for showing the details of this Japanese spec interior (the reason for the steering wheel on the right). It is a combination of marker and chalk on Bond paper. One-point perspective is all you need for a sketch such as this. Once I have an outline of the interior, I go from light to dark so that I can build up the values. Once again, you can always go darker, but you usually can't get lighter. Vignette helps transition out of the sketch, and in this case helped to keep me from having to render in the rear seats. Yet, it gives you their placement relative to the rest of the layout.

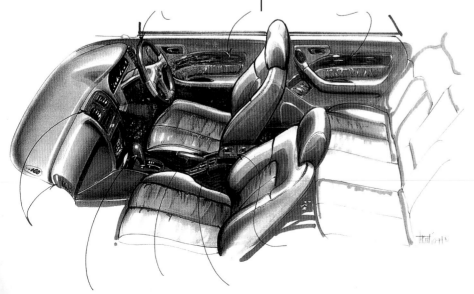

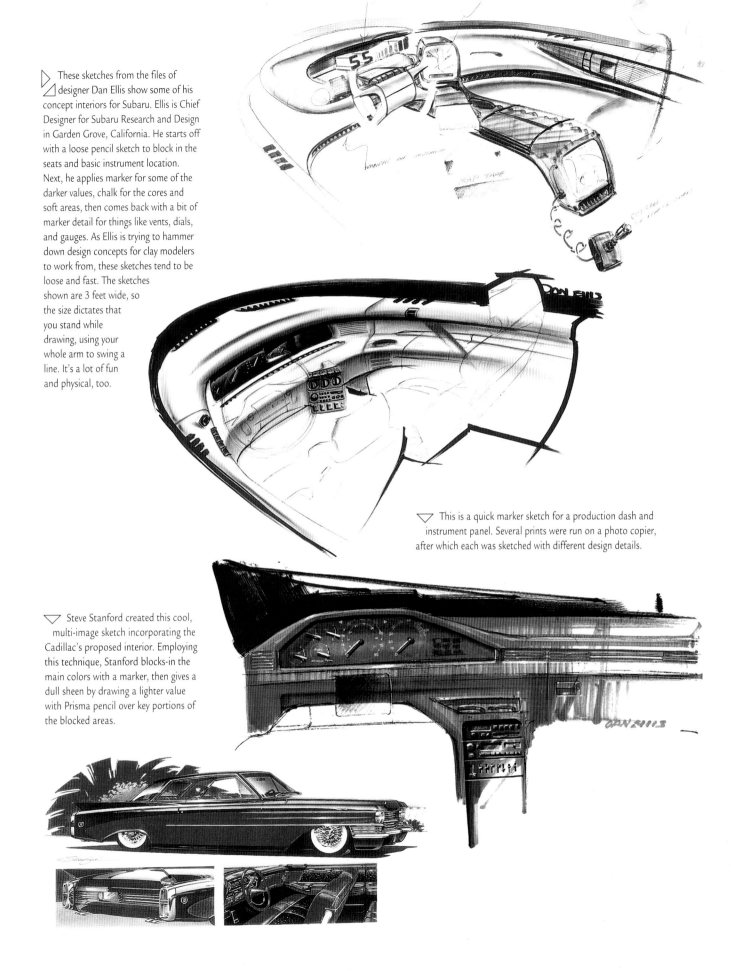

▷ These sketches from the files of designer Dan Ellis show some of his concept interiors for Subaru. Ellis is Chief Designer for Subaru Research and Design in Garden Grove, California. He starts off with a loose pencil sketch to block in the seats and basic instrument location. Next, he applies marker for some of the darker values, chalk for the cores and soft areas, then comes back with a bit of marker detail for things like vents, dials, and gauges. As Ellis is trying to hammer down design concepts for clay modelers to work from, these sketches tend to be loose and fast. The sketches shown are 3 feet wide, so the size dictates that you stand while drawing, using your whole arm to swing a line. It's a lot of fun and physical, too.

▽ This is a quick marker sketch for a production dash and instrument panel. Several prints were run on a photo copier, after which each was sketched with different design details.

▽ Steve Stanford created this cool, multi-image sketch incorporating the Cadillac's proposed interior. Employing this technique, Stanford blocks-in the main colors with a marker, then gives a dull sheen by drawing a lighter value with Prisma pencil over key portions of the blocked areas.

Computers

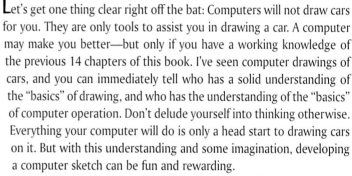

Let's get one thing clear right off the bat: Computers will not draw cars for you. They are only tools to assist you in drawing a car. A computer may make you better—but only if you have a working knowledge of the previous 14 chapters of this book. I've seen computer drawings of cars, and you can immediately tell who has a solid understanding of the "basics" of drawing, and who has the understanding of the "basics" of computer operation. Don't delude yourself into thinking otherwise. Everything your computer will do is only a head start to drawing cars on it. But with this understanding and some imagination, developing a computer sketch can be fun and rewarding.

As a tool, the computer becomes another medium you can use to create. Just as a pencil sketch, pastel rendering, or oil painting gives a unique look to your work, so, too, will a computer. It offers you choices and looks for your illustrations that could never have been achieved with a pencil, brush, or "real-world" tools.

So let's say you know the proper way to draw cars, but you love computers and would like to combine that love with your knowledge of drawing cars. How do you do it? There are three basic ways to do a drawing on a computer. One is by sketching your car on paper and scanning it into the computer. Then you come into the scan and can clean up your lines, manipulate them, or leave them alone and render-in the sketch with color or gray tones. Different finishes can be applied to each component or body surface. Some programs have filters that can apply an

Jim Bruni's computer art for this champagne label/poster combines the best of layout, color, and rendering. Taken as a whole, it appears to be an awesome undertaking but is actually composed of a series of sub-assemblies all tied together. Some of those are broken down here. And you already know how to render a car like this in regular media because you've read the book this far, right?

1959 TALBOT-LAGO T 150C-SS POURTOUT COUPE — TWO-TIME RECIPIENT OF THE PEBBLE BEACH CONCOURS D'ELEGANCE FRENCH CUP

116

△ This is Bruni's first thumbnail for layout purposes. Even the client doesn't see these. These get refined with color markers or Prisma pencils and become a roadmap for the illustration to follow.

"airbrush" or "painted" look to your illustration. The finishing touch can be a scanned or drawn background.

The second way is to use a pressure-sensitive digitized pad and stylus. With this equipment, you can sketch your car right on the screen by pressing the stylus on the pressure pad. In this way, you are actually drawing with the computer. Increased pressure from the stylus on the pad increases the line weights or emphasis of the line work. As you will see in some of Ed Golden's illustrations, there are other things these stylus and pad components allow an artist to do. Good eye-to-hand coordination is essential here, so all of those computer action games you wasted your time with in your youth may finally come in handy! The sketch is then finished off in the same manner as the scanned pencil sketch in the previous example.

The third way is to scan in a photo and manipulate it, which may or may not result in a photo-realistic depiction, but only if you understand the basics of drawing. It can be very rudimentary at best, unless you take it further. Again, some of Golden's examples give you an idea of what the computer can do in the hands of someone who chooses to explore this method of illustration. You can have fun with the photo manipulation, but when you get serious it is best to understand how to draw to achieve some really great art from your computer.

The software scene is changing all of the time, but some programs are almost staples for computer drawing and design. Macintosh is the gorilla of the computer graphics trade, and there are several versions of Freehand and Photoshop. For IBM-compatible personal computers, there is CorelDraw. There are more, but these will definitely get you just about everywhere you want to go.

Those interested in computers will likely use a PC for experimentation, but the "big boys" have bigger computer "toys." Alias Research and Evans & Sutherland are two companies that provide computer systems specifically for the professional auto designer. These systems create and render forms in 3-D. They can pass reflections over the car's surface to give the impression that the sketch is actually moving, while allowing the viewer to see the image from different perspectives in one fluid movement. Once the sketch is approved, the information is transferred to a stereolithography system where the image is created in model form. In this way, you eliminate the need to have someone physically model the car you have just sketched. The images can also be fed into a CAD/CAM for engineering and tooling. These are the true benefits to computer-drawn images. Plus, it gives the designer more information and flexibility, while allowing him to see his work in a whole new way. Most companies

▽ All of the tree-like, leafy background goodies were worked out in pencil and then scanned in. Once entered into digital form, you can flip-flop, clone, and distort the scanned tracing. The software's capabilities allow you to use these leaf elements to fill out the background, as well as the tree shadow on the ground, and the reflection in the top surfaces, and windshield of the car.

◁ The pencil rough for the woman was scanned into the Freehand illustration program. This is a guide for entering the linework, with values, colors, and line weights all added to the image by aid of the computer.

Software: Painting vs. Postscript

The following is a brief background on the distinction between painting and Postscript program software. These programs have to do with how the computer thinks of your art. Just as you would approach a pencil illustration differently than a marker sketch, the ways you create with these programs will differ.

Painting Programs

A painting program stores a map of your image in its memory and updates it as you work; it treats it like a complex mosaic. The software remembers the exact location (top to bottom and left to right) of each "tile" of the mosaic. It records the exact hue, intensity, and value of each bit or pixel, and an average image can contain hundreds of thousands of them. As you work on your illustration, you alter this bitmap by "painting" new values over old. The computer remembers each change, pixel by pixel. Subtle changes in these values can produce soft-edge effects like airbrush, smear, and blur. This natural, "soft" feeling is often characteristic of work created with paint programs. High-end software such as Adobe Photoshop or Fractal Design Painter keep track of images using this complex memory-intensive pixel-by-pixel method, so it's best to use these programs on a computer with plenty of RAM (random access memory) so they can work efficiently.

Postscript Programs

Postscript programs, on the other hand, create what are called object-oriented graphics. Postscript, by Adobe Systems, is the dominant object-oriented page description language in the graphic arts industry. When you draw a circle in one of the Postscript-based programs, the computer doesn't remember it as a map of dots. Instead, it remembers that you drew an object—a circle of fixed size and fill and outline. The other gigantic Postscript advantage over painting programs is apparent when it comes time to print your work. Since Postscript programs keep track of the shapes and colors in your illustration as a series of mathematical formulae, the image has no fixed resolution—no pixels! This is called resolution independence, and it means you can enlarge and print out your image on as large a Postscript printer as you can find or afford. Not only that, but your illustration can be produced at that printer's best resolution, sharp as a tack, without any loss of definition. Make it billboard-size if you like!

On the other hand, a chief constraint in creating object-oriented graphics concerns those self-same objects that Postscript keeps track of. Each must have a single hard edge—the computer can only remember the formula for each object's shape, color, and outline characteristic. An easy way to think of how Postscript illustration works is to visualize your image as if you were creating a collage by cutting shapes out of colored paper and pasting them over each other. With that in mind, it's easy to see that the illustrations you'll create with a Postscript program will often have a hard-edged look to them. Soft and fuzzy is possible when using Postscript programs, but it takes some planning.

Postscript drawing programs like Macromedia Freehand and Adobe Illustrator produce the kind of work you see in package design, line art, album covers, and technical drawings.

No matter how you create illustrations with a computer, you should consider a scanner as essential equipment. The flatbed scanner is a second cousin to the copier, and it's the chief way of bringing your rough sketches and reference material into your illustration and onto your screen. Speaking of screens—the bigger the better. Some graphic artists even use two screens—one for the illustrations and one as sort of an electronic tabouret upon which to park the inevitable palettes, menus, and reference scraps that accumulate during the illustration process. They retrieve this stuff by merely "dragging" from one monitor to the other using the mouse or stylus.

Jim Bruni

▷ The background layer is made up entirely of gray values. The area behind the cars was simply scanned in and repeated with flip-flops and distortion.

▷ Both cars are made up of blue, orange, red, and shades. This shows the combined background and No. 48 car.

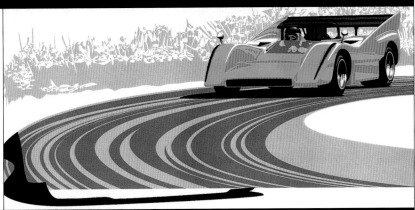

◁ With the No. 5 car layered in, this really takes on some life. Note that Bruni decided at this point to add some caution stripes in gray to the inside turn. From here, he added the lettering, graphics, and type to complete the illustration.

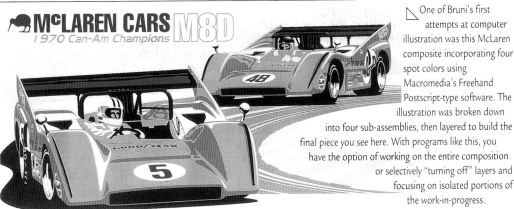

McLAREN CARS M8D
1970 Can-Am Champions

▷ One of Bruni's first attempts at computer illustration was this McLaren composite incorporating four spot colors using Macromedia's Freehand Postscript-type software. The illustration was broken down into four sub-assemblies, then layered to build the final piece you see here. With programs like this, you have the option of working on the entire composition or selectively "turning off" layers and focusing on isolated portions of the work-in-progress.

△ This book jacket
for Mark Dees'
incredible book on
racing legend Harry
Miller was created
entirely on the
computer by Bruni
using Macromedia's
Freehand Postscript
program. With this
program, the drawing is
done by a "points and
paths" method.

△ This book jacket for Mark Dees' incredible book on racing legend Harry Miller was created entirely on the computer by Bruni using Macromedia's Freehand Postscript program. With this program, the drawing is done by a "points and paths" method.

that hire artists and designers—from Ford Motor Company to Mattel to Industrial Light and Magic—incorporate these professional computer systems.

On these pages, you will see the work of two incredible computer artists. Ed Golden is a chief designer for Ford who took up computer sketching for business purposes, but also for fun and relaxation. He became almost obsessed with it and has mastered many programs to allow him to create in a way entirely different from the way he does in the Ford studios. Jim Bruni is an award-winning designer who has created all types of wheeled vehicles imaginable—from cars to wheelchairs—for clients such as Yamaha, Renault, Volvo, GM, Subaru, Nissan, Ford, and Universal Studios.

Some of their explanations may seem tedious and involved, but so does changing a tire when you read the steps broken down this way. In practice, these sketches were a lot easier to do.

Although your desktop computer is only a tool, it is the way things are being done today. As with any tool, it is only limited by the imagination of its user. Hopefully, the examples shown in this chapter will show you a few of the capabilities the computer holds for its user. With your knowledge of car drawing and your imagination enhanced with the capabilities of the computer, you should already be well into the twenty-first century.

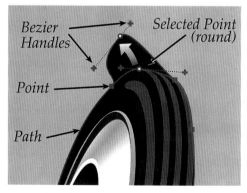

△ In this enlarged wheel detail, the path representing the silhouette of the tire has been selected and pulled outward like taffy. The path is defined by points (the little squares) that become visible when the path is selected. To modify the shape of any path, you merely "grab" and move any of its points. Selecting a point also causes its "bezier handles" to appear. By grabbing and moving these handles, the artist can fine-tune the curve between adjacent points. Once mastered, this technique gives the artist subtle and refined control.

◁ First, conventional pencil roughs are used to experiment with how the illustration and typography will work with the proportions and format of the book jacket. Going through this step on the computer is simply not as intuitive and can lead to results that are stilted and lacking in spontaneity.

▷ A preliminary drawing is then created with "paths" representing the basic outline and details of the car. These can be modified at any time in the illustration process.

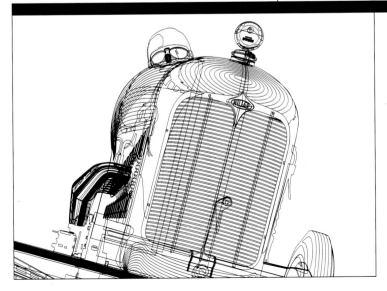

◁ This enlarged detail depicted in Freehand's keyline mode shows the repeating concentric paths that transition across the top of the hood and around the nose. A postscript program has the ability to compute these intermediate steps between any two selected paths of differing values. This capability enables the artist to achieve controlled gradations and airbrush-like blends.

▽ For Ed Golden's 1957 Chevy illustration, he started by scanning in a 1957 Chevy photo, then made a duplicate from which he removed the background. This was merged with a new, all-white layer that was created below the image. With all of this saved, another all-white layer is made, then placed on top of the image and made transparent to about 40 percent of its opacity so that you can see the original through it. The image now has a milky or fogged look. By removing sections of the transparent top layer, a "sketched" marker look can be achieved with a pressure-sensitive tool set to mimic a felt-tip marker in reverse. The eraser brush is set to give a marker look, removing white to block-in masses of high-contrast, solid color that are actually the base of the illustration. You are "drawing" by actually removing white that blocks your view of the original. The transparency of the top layer on which you are working can be shifted back to full opacity for comparison at any time. If too much white has been removed, it can be reinstated by simply switching from eraser to paint brush and filling an area of the top layer with white again. This makes for a very flexible and forgiving technique conducive to experimentation. Now, a second version of the eraser brush is needed that will mimic the look of chalk. Save the status of the illustration before switching from the "marker" brush to the "chalk" brush, because once work has begun with the chalk brush, restoration of the original is more difficult. The chalk brush is created from the eraser brush with almost the opposite attributes of the "marker" setting. This version should have no solid core and a very soft edge. Ideally, a diameter of 5 to 10 times from the previous brush is wanted. The overall opacity removed by each stroke should be very light, say 10 to 20 percent, so that total removal requires about 10 passes. This allows the gradations of color to gradually build as the white layer is slowly removed. Again, you are "drawing" simply by removing the white a little at a time. The trick is to not remove too much white, revealing too much of the original's detail, thus making the photo recognizable for what it is. To finalize the illustration, the top layer is adjusted to near 100 percent opacity and saved. Post-illustration tricks like color change or substitution, posterizing, or various filter effects can lead the illustration even further away from its original photo look.

The technique for this Formula 1 car is the same as described for the 1957 Chevy. The background of the finished illustration was changed from white to a gradated color. The entire image was then manipulated in Photoshop with a variety of experiments with color, hue, and contrast to arrive at the final look. Note that the details of the sponsor's decals did not have to be laboriously added as they were already in the original photo.

For this sketch, Golden wanted to focus on the rear of the car and vignette the image as it moves away. Note that the front wheel and fender were indicated with very little detail incorporating spontaneous brush or marker indication. Although the strokes appear loose or sloppy, they accentuate the design and form of the car.

This illustration was created with a vector graphic or "draw" software program like Adobe Illustrator, Macromedia Freehand, or Deneba's Canvas. A reference photo was scanned and opened in Freehand, then placed into its own separate layer for reference only. With the reference photo visible, basic shapes and forms are created in numerous layers to create a simplified version of the car. By applying Metatools' Vector Effects "Sketch" filter, Golden was able to "loosen up" the stiff, precise nature of the linework. Applying the Sketch filter instantly warps and offsets the shapes that were drawn and simultaneously renders borders or "sketch lines" around those shapes. These two features are fully adjustable in a preview window in Vector Effects, allowing a full range of looks from subtle all the way to unrecognizable, all at the push of a button.

△ This concept car sketch was designed by Evans & Sutherland using their Conceptual Design and Rendering Software, or CDRS. The sketch suggests a theme for a future Ford Mustang that draws on the original 1965 design.

▽ Here we have an image that demonstrates how a new version of CDRS called PerspectaSketch was used to create an early 3-D model from the previous 2-D sketch. With PerspectaSketch, a designer can create a 3-D surface model by simply drawing lines over a hand-drawn or painted 2-D perspective sketch. With literally a single menu pick, the system automatically converts 2-D curves into 3-D curves and surfaces them.

Schools

If you are truly interested in drawing cars or products—I mean really consumed by it—or have always wanted to dream up cool spaceships or creatures for movies, and you have sustained that interest in spite of this book, then a next possible step is to look into enrolling in a professional school that caters to automotive or product design.

Think about it: Every product from a TV zapper to a semi-truck needs to be designed. That means it needs to be drawn. There are schools that teach this process and lay a strong career foundation. In the United States there are two colleges that have a great reputation for this type of education. Art Center College of Design in Pasadena, California, and Center For Creative Studies (CCS) in Detroit, Michigan, are famous for their graduates making up the bulk of designer staffs in the automotive, consumer product, and toy designing fields.

Both Art Center and CCS are accredited four-year colleges that provide you with the necessary skills and training to forge a career in automotive and product design and design for the movie industry. They utilize working professionals who take time to teach, so you are instructed by those who are in the field of design and who probably have degrees from

▷ Art Center's campus in the hills overlooking Pasadena, California, provides a professional atmosphere with teachers who are working professionals in their given design or art major. It is a fully accredited college, with graduates receiving a Bachelor of Science degree in Transportation Design upon completion of the eight-semester curriculum. *Steven A. Heller/Art Center College of Design*

the very school at which they teach. All aspects of design are covered, with an emphasis on conceptual drawing and visualization. I am a graduate of Art Center and have taught there, too, so I'm a firm believer in going this direction if you are really serious about doing this type of work. The big restriction will be cost; these schools aren't cheap! Grants at the high school level are one avenue to pursue, and student loans have become almost mandatory for the costs involved.

Additionally, there are state colleges that have automotive or product design classes: Cleveland Institute of Art in Ohio and Wayne State in Detroit, Michigan. Obviously, you should do the research on all the schools you have an interest in attending. Keep in mind that some colleges continue to get into the process of design, without getting into the actual conceptualization of a product or car. That's O.K., but ask to see completed projects and models. If they hand you a notebook of diagrams, research, and a few pictures, look elsewhere. The research and marketing of a product are very important parts of the design process, but you want to draw and design, right?

If you are in high school and think this field is where you want to be, I know that Art Center has Saturday classes for high school-level students. This can be a terrific way to get professional training early on, and it also gives you a chance to work in the school's unique environment. It may initially be intimidating, but can quickly become intoxicating, what with all the other projects and activities going on at the school. It gives you insight to the comings and goings of the students, and exposes you to lots of excellent student work. Unfortunately, this only works for Southern Californians, or those who choose to relocate there, since the school is in Pasadena.

Regardless of the level of your education, if you're still in school, it would be a good idea to take as many art classes as possible. Tell the instructor your particular interest is drawing or designing cars, and ask if you can get some help and be allowed to pursue that goal. Most teachers are eager to help when a student has a specific objective and shows some initiative.

The addresses for these two institutions:

Art Center College of Design
1700 Lida St.
Pasadena, CA 91103-1999

Center For Creative Studies
245 E. Kirby
Detroit, MI 48202

△ Advanced-term Transportation Design students are shown thrashing for the Mitsubishi project final presentation. Completed projects are reviewed by the company sponsor and can include 3-D models, development sketches, and final renderings. In some cases, full-size renderings are also required. All the major automobile companies sponsor projects, giving students a chance to work in conditions similar to real-world design constraints. Center For Creative Studies in Detroit, Michigan, holds similar company-sponsored competitions. *Steven A. Heller/Art Center College of Design*

Since its inception, the automobile has been that object of promise, adventure, freedom, beauty, lust, and mystery. Almost everybody owns one. Almost everybody wants one. And it's up to a new generation of designers and illustrators to carry the torch that was ignited by many brilliant and creative talents during the twentieth century.

Your job is to put the twenty-first century into a car that will perpetuate the American Dream. One that looks good, feels good, and performs better than its forefathers. Good luck.

Appendix
The designers who contributed

Mark Balfe
1230 Bryant Ave. S., #11
So. St. Paul, MN 55075

Dave Bell
1834 Asbury St. N.
St. Paul, MN 55113

John Bell
554 19th Ave.
San Francisco, CA 94121

Jim Bruni
401 Le Droit Lane
Laguna Beach, CA 92651

Dave "Big" Deal
1651 Monte Vista Dr.
Vista, CA 92084

Dan Ellis
Chief Designer, Subaru Research and Design
Garden Grove, California

Ed Golden
Chief Designer, Ford Motor Co.
Dearborn, Michigan

Darrell Mayabb
10180 W. 73rd Place
Arvada, CO 80005

Ed Newton
P.O. Box 1034
Dublin, OH 43017

Charlie Smith
c/o Radhaus Inc.
P.O. Box 16102
Kansas City, MO 64112

Lance Sorchik
16 White Oak Dr.
Sussex, NJ 07461

Steve Stanford
7416 Westminster Blvd.
Westminster, CA 92683

Thom Taylor
P.O. Box 3271
Dana Point, CA 92629-9998

Greg Tedder
24782 Thornberry Circle
Moreno Valley, CA 92387

Tom West
621 Rushing Creek Place
Thousand Oaks, CA 91360

Index